THE SCOUT LAW
IN ACTION

THE SCOUT LAW
IN ACTION

Compiled by WALTER MacPEEK

ABINGDON PRESS   ♪   Nashville   New York

The Scout Law in Action

Copyright © 1966 by Abingdon Press

ISBN 0-687-37028-0

Library of Congress Catalog Card Number: 66-21966

We express our indebtedness to all who contributed to this compilation and our appreciation to the Boy Scouts of America and to others for permission to reprint material: the Editorial Service, *Boys' Life*, and *Scouting Magazine*.

"A Prayer," by Frank Dempster Sherman, used by permission of Houghton Mifflin Co. "Pass It On," by Henry Burton, from *Masterpieces of Religious Verse*, ed. by James Dalton Morrison, by permission of Harper & Row, Publishers.

SET UP, PRINTED, AND BOUND BY THE
PARTHENON PRESS, AT NASHVILLE,
TENNESSEE, UNITED STATES OF AMERICA

Dedicated to
my wife and son
and to all good Scouts and
Scouters who have helped
to make the Scout Law
more real and meaningful
to me

THE SCOUT OATH

On my honor I will do my best
To do my duty to God and my country
and to obey the Scout Law;
To help other people at all times;
To keep myself physically strong,
mentally awake, and morally straight.

THE SCOUT LAW

A Scout is
TRUSTWORTHY
A Scout's honor is to be trusted. If he were to violate his honor by telling a lie or by cheating or by not doing exactly a given task, when trusted on his honor, he may be directed to hand over his Scout badge.

LOYAL
He is loyal to all to whom loyalty is due, his Scout leader, his home and parents and country.

HELPFUL
He must be prepared at any time to save life, help injured persons, and share the home duties. He must do at least one Good Turn to somebody every day.

FRIENDLY
He is a friend to all and a brother to every other Scout.

COURTEOUS
He is polite to all, especially to women, children, old people, and the weak and helpless. He must not take pay for being helpful or courteous.

KIND
He is a friend to animals. He will not kill nor hurt any living creature needlessly, but will strive to save and protect all harmless life.

OBEDIENT

He obeys his parents, Scoutmaster, patrol leader and all other duly constituted authorities.

CHEERFUL

He smiles whenever he can. His obedience to orders is prompt and cheery. He never shirks nor grumbles at hardship.

THRIFTY

He does not wantonly destroy property. He works faithfully, wastes nothing, and makes the best use of his opportunities. He saves his money so that he may pay his own way, be generous to those in need, and helpful to worthy objects. He may work for pay, but must not receive tips for courtesies or Good Turns.

BRAVE

He has the courage to face danger in spite of fear and to stand up for the right against the coaxings of friends or the jeers or threats of enemies, and defeat does not down him.

CLEAN

He keeps clean in body and thought; stands for clean speech, clean sport, clean habits; and travels with a clean crowd.

REVERENT

He is reverent toward God. He is faithful in his religious duties and respects the convictions of others in matters of custom and religion.

FOREWORD

The use of the twelve points of the Scout Law can be made vital guideposts in a boy's growth. The boy who has been a Scout for one day knows something of what it means, for instance, to be trustworthy. But a month later he should be able to better understand the concept. The concept should grow clearer with the passage of time. Two months later—providing he has had actual experience in trustworthiness in troop and patrol—he should be still more devoted to the ideal, and skilled in the everyday practice of being trustworthy.

HOW THE LEADER CAN HELP

The Scoutmaster can focus attention upon and emphasize the points of the Scout Law in various ways:

- through living them in his personal life;

• through helping boys to understand the implications of the various points of the Law;

• through helping boys to feel more strongly committed to observance of the Law;

• and in numerous other ways.

EMPHASIZING A POINT A MONTH

One Scoutmaster has worked out the plan of emphasizing a different point of the Law each month. This troop follows the calendar year. In January the emphasis is upon "A Scout is Trustworthy." In February they focus upon "A Scout is Loyal." And so throughout the year.

Every Scout in the troop is expected to learn or to relearn the "fine print" on that one point of the Law that month. At patrol leaders' council early in January the Scoutmaster shares with the patrol leaders the best anecdotes he can find illustrating trustworthiness in action. Patrol leaders are invited to tell of any appropriate incidents with which they are familiar.

Then the Scoutmaster asks, "How can we work these ideas into activities? Are there any situations that we can set up in meetings or in camp that will emphasize, encourage, or test our Scouts' understanding and use of this point of the Law?"

This Scoutmaster reports that his patrol leaders

are very much in earnest in helping to make the Law take hold in the lives of the Scouts in the troop.

POSITIVE INTERPRETATION

Sometimes a boy brings a clipping or an anecdote or other incident that shows the results of someone who has failed to be trustworthy. We prefer the positive, and we continually encourage Scouts to look for positive incidents rather than negative ones. However, even in an incident of failure to use a point of the Law, there is the suggestion of happier results that are obtained by using it.

BULLETIN BOARD

"We have a special bulletin board with the point of the Law being emphasized that month nicely lettered at the top. Our boys bring photographs, clippings, quotations, whatever they think will help us to understand what that point of the Law means," a Scoutmaster explains.

A TOOL TO USE

The twelve points of the Scout Law are often repeated. But we need to go deeper than merely saying the words. We need to help boys grasp the meaning and feel the compelling need to use those points of the Law as guides for action in their daily lives.

How can you as a Scoutmaster help to dramatize the points of the Scout Law? How can you enlist the help of your patrol leaders to make the Law come alive in the actions of your Scouts? Only you can give the answer.

The collection of illustrations in this book may help you. But in the final analysis, what counts most is the personal life lived by the Scouters of your troop, and the program of action in patrol and troop that gives Scouts actual experience in coming to better understand, to feel concern for, and to put the twelve points of the Scout Law into daily practice in their lives.

WALTER MacPEEK
North Brunswick, New Jersey

CONTENTS

1. A Scout Is Trustworthy 15

2. A Scout is Loyal 27

3. A Scout Is Helpful 42

4. A Scout Is Friendly 55

5. A Scout Is Courteous 69

6. A Scout Is Kind 76

7. A Scout Is Obedient 87

8. A Scout Is Cheerful 94

9. A Scout Is Thrifty 101

10. A Scout Is Brave 111

11. A Scout Is Clean 121

12. A Scout Is Reverent 128

Index 143

1

A Scout Is Trustworthy

A Scout's honor is to be trusted.
If he were to violate his honor
. . . by telling a lie,
. . . or by cheating,
. . . or by not doing exactly a
  given task,
. . . when trusted on his honor,
. . . he may be directed
  to hand over his Scout badge.

A SCOUT IS TRUSTWORTHY

He is worth trusting.

A clock or a watch that doesn't tell the truth is more bother than it is worth. It can't be trusted. But a real Scout can.

Honor! Integrity! Dependability!

Those are power-packed words and power-packed qualities in a Scout's life.

15

"Doing exactly a given task . . . when trusted on his honor."

Think of the integrity of Washington and Franklin and of many others. Think of our rich and varied heritages, none of them more precious, none more significant, than the examples of those men who demonstrated a high sense of personal integrity.

"You may trust him in the dark." —*Cicero*

"To be trusted is a greater compliment than to be loved."—*George MacDonald*

"Aaron Burr was a more brilliant man than George Washington. If he had been loyal to truth, he would have been an abler man; but that which made George Washington the chief hero in our great republic was the sagacity, not of intellectual genius, but of the moral element in him."   —*A. E. Dunning*

IF YOU WILL STEAL

When Theodore Roosevelt was a ranchman, one of his cowboys triumphantly put the "R" brand on a maverick which had strayed in from a neighbor's enclosure. The future President dismissed him on the spot. "If you steal *for* me," was his blunt explanation, "you will steal *from* me."

HE BUILT A HOUSE

A young carpenter was hired by his elderly father, who had suddenly become rich, to build a new house. After providing enough money to buy the best materials, the old man went away on a long trip. The son was soon to be married and saw a chance to get some extra money for himself. Instead of doing an honest job he erected an attractive-looking house in a cheap way by using secondhand lumber and putting a poor grade of cement in the foundation. He was sure his father would not know the difference.

When the old man returned he said, "The house is your wedding present, my son. I wanted you to build it to suit yourself since you are to live in it."
—*Walter D. Cavert*

MEN PUT THEIR TRUST IN HIM

I went to a bank president whom I knew, and who knew me. I remember perfectly how anxious I was to get that loan and to establish myself favorably with the banker. This gentleman was T. P. Handy, a gentle old man, well-known as a man of character.

For fifty years he had been interested in young men. He had known me as a boy in the Cleveland schools. I gave him all the particulars of our business, telling him frankly about our affairs—what we wanted to use the money for. I waited for the verdict with almost trembling eagerness.

"How much do you want?" he said.

"Two thousand dollars."

"All right, Mr. Rockefeller, you can have it," he replied. "Just give me your own warehouse receipts; they're good enough for me."

As I left that bank, my elation can hardly be imagined. I held up my head—think of it, a bank had trusted me for two thousand dollars! I felt that I was now a man of importance in the community.

—*J. D. Rockefeller* in
THE PRACTICE OF THE OATH AND LAW

A FRESH START

A boy had lied to his father. What made it especially bad was that his father was also his Scout-master. The father was deeply hurt.

"I've never known you to lie to me before," he told his son. "Give me your tenderfoot badge."

Reluctantly his son silently unfastened his badge and handed it to his father. The father took the shining badge, placed it on the cement shelf, and struck it with a hammer. Two blows demolished it. The father showed no anger.

The Scout felt badly—way down deep inside. After all, he had done wrong and he was ashamed. What his father had done was only fair.

Several weeks later his father said to him, "Let's try again," and he pinned a shiny new badge on his son's shirt.

"I wanted my boy to make a clean break—to start with a clean slate."

The past was forgotten with the old badge. The boy got a fresh start with his new badge.

—Walter MacPeek

HIS WORD WAS GOOD

The code of honor in force among the boatmen of the Mississippi River in early days was crude but strict. There was the case of Bill McCloy, who fell into the clutches of the law. Brought before one of the courts at Natchez, he was committed to jail. The vacation of the court was just beginning and, unless McCloy could find a bondsman for ten thousand dollars, he must swelter in jail throughout the long summer months. At the last moment Colonel W., a wealthy citizen of Natchez, came to the rescue, and agreed to pay ten thousand dollars if McCloy did not present himself to stand trial in the fall.

In vain the Colonel's friends tried to persuade

him not to take the responsibility; even the court's advice that he let the matter alone was unheeded. McCloy was released, shouldered his rifle, and in due time reached his home in "Old Kaintuck." The time of the trial approached. Everywhere the chances of McCloy's return were discussed. The Colonel had not heard from him since his departure.

The morning of the appointed day came, but the prisoner did not present himself. The court transacted its other business and was on the point of adjourning when McCloy, his beard long and matted, his hands scarred and bleeding, rushed into the courtroom.

Colonel W. embraced him as if he were a long-lost brother, and eyes unused to tears filled to overflowing when McCloy told his story.

Starting from Louisville as a "hand" on a flatboat he found in a few days that, owing to unexpected delays, he could not reach Natchez at the appointed time. No other craft presented itself, and so McCloy abandoned the flatboat and with the aid of rough tools shaped a canoe from the trunk of a fallen tree. He paddled his canoe, with only the briefest stops for food and rest, thirteen hundred miles, and redeemed his promise almost at the expense of his life.

His trial became a mere form; his chivalrous conduct and the want of any positive testimony won for him a quick verdict of "not guilty."

—TRUE STORIES OF REAL SCOUTS

IMPORTANCE OF KNOWING HOW

Sometimes an apparently little thing becomes very important. Some years ago there was a boy who wanted to be a Scout. His knot requirement gave him a lot of trouble. He practiced until he could produce a knot that passed inspection, but he knew that he had not really mastered the sheet bend.

After he had joined the troop, some of the things his Scoutmaster had said to him about the first point of the Law made him think. Entirely on his own he practiced his Tenderfoot knots till he knew he was qualified. Then came his real test.

A steeplejack, by a series of accidents, was stranded at nightfall on a chimney two hundred feet in the air with no way to get down. He was exhausted and unnerved and could not hold on to his dangerous perch much longer.

His tackle was on the ground, but he remembered that ropes were too short, and he had not spliced them. He called down to the crowd to ask if anyone could make a knot that would hold. There was silence.

Then someone called, "Here comes a Boy Scout."

The Scout called up that he could make a sheet bend and tied the knot.

The tackle was sent up to the steeplejack by the lead rope. The steeplejack went over the edge in his "chair" and prayed all the way down that the Scout knew what he was doing.

The steeplejack reached the ground safely. The crowd cheered and shook his hand. But one member of the crowd was nearly in tears. It was the Tenderfoot Scout who had tied the sheet bend and saved the life.   —Boy Scout Handbook

PRIDE IN WORK

Years ago a chair manufacturer employed a large group of young men to make chairs by hand. He paid his men according to how many chairs they made each week, but tested the chairs and paid for only those that were well made—those that passed certain tests.

The owner of the factory kept his eye on two young men—Rufas and Henry. Each turned out a good number of chairs each week and very rarely did either of them have a chair fail to be approved. As time went on the factory owner needed a section superintendent. He might choose Rufas or he might choose Henry.

How do you think he went about making the

decision? He assembled all the men and announced that they would be paid for all the chairs they made regardless of whether they passed inspection or not.

What do you suppose happened? Yes—many more chairs were made and the percentage of poor ones increased greatly.

However the factory owner checked the chairs which Henry and Rufas made. All the chairs Rufas made were as good as before. Half of Henry's chairs failed to be ok'd.

You guess who was advanced to the supervisor job.
—The Scoutmaster's Minute

TELLING THE TRUTH

Just why is it important to tell the truth? Sure, a Scout promises to be trustworthy, and telling the truth is a big part of what we mean by being trustworthy. And of course a Scout tells the truth since he has promised that he will do his best to live up to all twelve points of the Scout Law, and being trustworthy is the first of them.

One of the best, clearest, easiest to understand statements on the importance of truth telling came out of the illness, some time ago, of the then President Eisenhower. It was in *This Week* magazine.

Merriman Smith, veteran United Press White House correspondent, asked President Eisenhower's press secretary, James Hagerty, in an interview, why nothing was held back about President Eisenhower's illness. Truth-telling in similar situations has not always been the policy followed.

Why was the truth told about Mr. Eisenhower's condition? Simply this: Ike told Hagerty to tell a straight story. Hagerty did. Smith asked him if he thought that was the best course of action they could have taken. Here's what Jim had to say; it's worth remembering. It helps all of us understand the importance of telling the truth.

These are his words: "There's nothing mysterious or clever about telling the truth. It is the greatest insurance policy ever invented, particularly in politics. A man in government, politics, or in any field of human relations who tries to lie out of a situation is bound to be found out sooner or later and seriously damaged, if not destroyed.

"And another thing, you don't have to trust your memory if you tell the truth."

—*Scoutmaster Art Webb*

NOT AN EASY TASK

When George Washington was a boy he lived with his mother on a plantation near Fredericksburg, Virginia, on the banks of the Rappahannock

River. His father, Augustine Washington, died when George was young.

Many stories of Washington's boyhood prove that the traits of character which made him such a great man were shaped while he was a boy.

One of these stories is about a sorrel colt which was a favorite of his mother. It was of good stock and, if properly trained, would make a fine, fast horse. But the colt was wild and vicious and resisted every effort to be broken.

One day George and several other boys were looking at the colt in the field and discussing its temperament. The boys declared that it could never be tamed, but George said: "You help me get on his back, and I'll tame him."

After much effort they got a bridle bit in the colt's mouth, and with George on its back it reared, kicked, and jumped. But it was finally subdued, and George rode the animal about the field. Then in one final effort to be free from the determined young rider on its back, the colt made such a desperate plunge that it burst a blood vessel and fell dead.

The boys were worried and tried to think of ways to evade the responsibility and consequences of their act. But George determined that the only right thing to do was to go straight to his mother and tell the truth. His mother heard his explanation and replied: "I am sorry to lose the colt, but I am proud to know that my son speaks the truth and does not try to put the blame for his acts upon others."

—*E. S. Brooks* in
TRUE STORIES OF GREAT AMERICANS

2

A Scout Is Loyal

He is loyal
... to all to whom loyalty is due—
... his Scout leader,
... his home and parents,
... and country.

What a challenging concept *loyalty* is! The very word makes us recall the motivating force of scores of great men who have built our nation. They were loyal to their group. They were loyal to the innate love of right within themselves. They were loyal to the highest they knew.

They reached high. They were men of loyal hearts reaching up to the highest of all law—right and justice and truth—sometimes in part, unknown, or and as yet undiscovered. But still they reached high.

Who loves me, follows me! —*Francis I*

It is better to be faithful than famous.
—Theodore Roosevelt

I only regret that I have but one life to lose for my country. —*Nathan Hale*

Our country is the common parent of us all.
—Cicero

To God, thy country, and thy friend be true.
—Vaughan

RELIVING AMERICA'S PIONEER DAYS

You know about Kit Carson and Lewis and Clark and Daniel Boone and all the dozens of adventurers and explorers who pushed the edges of civilization westward.

You admire the rugged pioneers who followed after those explorers and settled the land and built the new country. Often the life of these pioneers was a lonely one, always a difficult one, and some, of course, turned back. But many stayed and built homes and schools and churches.

Scouting experiences help you to understand more about the past—the pioneer days of our community and our nation. And through this understanding of days gone by we are able to relive again the life of our pioneer forefathers and to appreciate more deeply the nation they helped to build for us.

—*Walter MacPeek*

A PATRIOTIC GIFT

One hundred years ago Solomon Willard, architect and builder, started something in East Boston that is not likely to be lost sight of very soon. He designed and built the Bunker Hill Monument. As a patriotic gift to this country he devoted eighteen years of his life to superintending the erection of that great shaft—without remuneration of any kind!

What this country needs most desperately is more Solomon Willards—men who have great ability coupled with great patriotism, men who are eager to give their best to their country and who are not primarily concerned with tapping the public till.

—*Marcus Strong* in
The Practice of the Oath and Law

LOYALTY TO A BROTHER

E. W. Cassels tells this story: One of two brothers fighting in the same company in France fell by a German bullet. The one who escaped asked permission of his officer to go and bring his brother in.

"He is probably dead," said the officer, "and there is no use in your risking your life to bring in his body."

But after further pleading the officer consented. Just as the soldier reached the lines with his brother on his shoulders, the wounded man died.

"There, you see," said the officer, "you risked your life for nothing."

"No," replied Tom. "I did what he expected of me, and I have my reward. When I crept up to him and took him in my arms, he said, 'Tom, I knew you would come—I just felt you would come.'"

There you have the gist of it all; somebody expects something fine and noble and unselfish of us; someone expects us to be faithful.

—The Practice of the Oath and Law

A SCOUT COMES THROUGH

Nearly a hundred Scouts were gathered one Monday morning waiting for the train to take them to camp, to the land of their heart's desire. One especially fine-looking lad, brimming over with fun and energy, for want of something better to do, reached up and pulled the bell cord in the waiting train.

A Scout leader standing by explained to a trainman that the cord had been pulled in error, then turned to the Scout and said severely: "Your Scout-master would be proud of you if he knew you were trying to cause trouble for the trainmen and give all Scouts a black eye, wouldn't he? Look at that Troop numeral on your sleeve. You're surely bringing a fine sort of credit to your Troop!"

The leader walked away, and the Scout looked out the window. A flush came over his face, and his companions sat very still.

A moment later the Scout was up near the front of the car saying to the leader, "I'm sorry, Sir. I really didn't mean to do that. I didn't know it would cause anybody any trouble. I'm really sorry. Don't blame my troop. It's my fault."

"That's all right, Son," the leader told him as they smiled at each other. "I like to see a fellow admit his error, face the music, and come through. You're a real Scout."

The boy went back to his companions, his happy young heart relieved now. The leader was pleased to have seen a boy build a victory out of what had started to be an unfortunate incident.

—Walter MacPeek

THE STORY OF GREYFRIARS' BOBBY

In 1858 a poor shepherd died and was buried in a graveyard at Edinburgh, Scotland, his only mourner being a little Skye terrier. On the two succeeding mornings the sexton found the dog lying on his master's grave and drove him away with hard words, dogs being against the rules of the cemetery.

The third morning was cold and wet, and when the sexton found him shivering on the newly made grave, he hadn't the heart to drive him away and gave him something to eat.

From that time the dog made the churchyard his home, every night for eleven years and three months. No matter how cold or wet or stormy the night, he could not be induced to stay away from the beloved spot, and if shut up would howl dismally.

Every day, when the castle gun was fired at ten o'clock, he went punctually to a restaurant nearby where the proprietor fed him. At one time Bobby was in great danger of being seized and done away with by the dogcatcher because his tax had not been paid. The boys and girls of the neighborhood collected the amount and tendered it to the Lord Provost. This official was so moved by what the children had done that he promise to stand good for Bobby and so exempted him from the dog tax, and to mark his admiration of his fidelity presented him with a handsome collar inscribed "Greyfriars' Bobby, presented by the Lord Provost of Edinburgh."

Bobby had many friends and visitors, and many, besides the men employed about the yard, tried to win his affections; but he refused to attach himself to any one person. For more than eleven years he kept watch over his master's humble grave, and then died quietly of old age and was buried in a flower plot nearby. A granite fountain was erected in 1872 to the memory of the homeless dog, and a bronze statue of Bobby stands on top of it. It was the gift of a kind and wealthy woman, Baroness Burdett Coutts, and may be seen to this day just outside the gate of the churchyard where Bobby's beloved master was buried—the spot that was watched and guarded by the faithful little dog to his dying day. Lady Coutts said she built the monument to Greyfriars' Bobby to teach the boys and girls of Edinburgh the meaning of such devotion.

—OUR DUMB ANIMALS

MEANING OF VALLEY FORGE

"What happened at Valley Forge back in the winter of 1777-78?"

Valley Forge is a memorial shrine which recalls days of deep despair, of stern privation and hardship. We picture the training of a ragged, hungry army, growing into a teamwork of power and spirit. The welding of the spirit of a struggling people was accomplished there.

The mention of Valley Forge brings to mind the names of von Steuben, De Kalb, Lafayette, Kosciusko, and others. But the great master heart of that bleak winter was George Washington—father of our country.

In later years Washington wrote, "Through the want of shoes and stockings and the hard frozen ground, you might have tracked the army from White Marsh to Valley Forge by the blood of their feet."

In those cold December days they pitched their tents on the ground about the Schuylkill River. During the period that they cut timber to build log huts, Washington insisted on living in a tent himself, and not until the soldiers were housed in wooden shelters did he take up his quarters in the Isaac Watts house.   —Walter MacPeek

HE STUCK TO HIS SHIP

A few years ago a quiet, unassuming man became known throughout the nation overnight because he refused to abandon his crippled ship.

They called him "Captain Stayput." He lived up to the tradition of the sea, that he would stay by his ship. Some of you may remember the admiration shown by newspaper headlines and widespread interest throughout the country and around the world.

Captain Kurt Carlson, a thirty-seven-year-old, shy and modest man from Woodbridge, New Jersey, wanted no special praise for his deeds. His strong sense of personal loyalty and duty kept him aboard his ship, the *Flying Enterprise*, after all others had abandoned it.

For nearly two weeks he remained on the deck as the ship rolled, stricken and disabled, in the heavy sea. He was determined to do everything he could to save his valuable cargo.

He failed to save his cargo, but he set an example of devotion to duty and sticking-by as long as it was humanly possible. Today many people remember his spirit; if he had not demonstrated such dependability he would have been forgotten long ago.

—THE SCOUTMASTER'S MINUTE

LIVING ON
(A quiet chat as the campfire dies down)

"Fellows, we've been sitting here tonight around the campfire. We watched it grow from a tiny flame to a blaze that shed its light and heat so that many of us drew back. Then the fire burned down, got lower and lower, and now it has almost burned

35

itself out. In another few hours this campfire will be entirely gone. But will it? Or will something of this campfire live on forever in our hearts—some feeling of friendliness or respect for one another— some feeling of faith in our world and in ourselves?

"If something that has been thought, or felt, or hoped for as we have gathered here at our campfire should change your world—even a little bit—then this campfire will live on, will not be finished with the dying down of the flame and the clearing away of the ashes.

"The influence of our entire Scouting experience is something like this. We may leave our old troop after a few years, may even cease to be members of the Boy Scouts of America, but something of the Scouting spirit inside us lives on—forever."

—*Walter MacPeek*

FATHER "TURNED AROUND"

Did you ever get turned around? I'll tell you a story about being turned around.

It was the first trip the boy ever made to the canyon. He went with his father. They left the ranch early in the morning and went away up into the tall quaking aspens.

Along in the afternoon they started back to the ranch. The boy was in high glee. He sat behind his father on the wagon, holding on the binder lever. As they rode down the canyon, horses on the trot, they made a sudden turn in the shape of a horseshoe. This turn gradually moved out on the other side of the canyon and on down the way.

The boy said to his father, after they had made the horseshoe curve: "Father, you are going wrong."

The father said, "Are we?"

He said, "Yes, don't you see?"

And the horses trotted on, and the boy looked this way and that way up and down, and said: "Pop, you are turned around."

And the father said, "Well, do you want to get off?"

And he said, "No, Pop, I'll stay with you."

On they went and the boy said, "Pop, the canyon is turned around." On they went, and finally they came around a little bend to a little opening that led up to the place where the ranch was, and he said, "We are straight again." As they got off the wagon he said, "Gee, Pop, I'm glad I stayed with you."

—George H. Brimhall

SHARING

In Constantinople where the great church of Saint Sophia stands, this is the legend of the way it received its name.

Back in the sixth century the Emperor Justinian

lived in Constantinople. He was a great emperor and a great builder; he built many things for his people—public buildings and fortresses that would stand for years. The emperor desired something that would become *his* monument, to be named for him, something that people would look upon and say, "Behold, this is the work of the Emperor Justinian."

He thought long about it and at last decided to erect a great church. No other hand, no other purse, was to be allowed to contribute toward its construction. His was to be the decision in every detail, his the provision for every expense.

Finally the last stone was lifted into place, and the day of dedication came. The crowd pressed close about the door, and Justinian drew back the veil. A shout of amazement burst from the crowd. For where the name of Justinian was to have been engraved was the name of an unknown woman.

"Who is this woman?" demanded the emperor. "Hunt her out and bring her here."

After a long search they brought her before the platform, a broken old woman, in tears. In halting sentences she sobbed out her story.

"I do not know how my name came to be written there; I gave no contribution to the temple; I am too poor for that. Only—one day as the oxen on their way to the temple went past my house, I saw how they were struggling under the load of heavy stones and I snatched a little straw from my mattress and held it up for them to eat."

That was all she had done—all that her poverty would allow her to do. But the angels who weigh the motives of men and women had written her name there instead of that of the emperor Justinian because, having nothing else to give, she had given as her heart had prompted her.

—*Author Unknown*

THE "WE" SPIRIT

Scouts, when I hear one of you refer to the management of a Scout troop in terms of "we," not "they," and "ours," not "theirs," I am pretty sure that you are experiencing significant values in scouting.

The "we" spirit is important in our Scout troop, school, community, business, and nation. The lawbreaker, the responsibility-dodger, and the glory-seeker talk in terms of "I" and "they," not "we" and "our."

Scouts, don't think for a minute that I'm talking about just choice of words. The pronouns are merely symptoms of our underlying ways of feeling and acting.

39

Have you ever heard conversations like these?

"How is the community fund drive going?"

"Way behind. They don't run it right in this town."

Or perhaps: "What about downtown parking facilities?"

"Aw, they don't think of anything till it's too late."

Or when asked about schools, someone might say, "They're nothing extra. They spend a lot of money and the kids can't even spell."

I hope you fellows talk about "our" and "we" with pride. In every way within our power we need to help people develop the "we" spirit. Boys need to start in Cub Scout dens to think and talk and feel and act in terms of "we" and "our." As the years go by and they come into our troop, they need to have more and more actual experience in helping make decisions and plans and programs, in having real experience on a "we" basis in "our" troop serving "our" community, better understanding "our" nation and "our" world.

I'm glad that you and I live in a "we" community in "our" America, and we're proud of "our" troop.

—*Walter MacPeek* in
THE SCOUTMASTER'S MINUTE

EARNING THE RIGHT TO BE A CITIZEN

"I am sorry, Bob, but you don't belong to this camp now. You'd better go over and sit under the tree while we go on with the game," the Camp Director spoke in a very impersonal tone, and if there was any warmth of feeling, his voice did not show it.

The boy looked at him quizzically.

"What do you mean, I don't belong?" he asked.

"I work only with those who are willing to play the game. You have been showing that you don't want to pull together with us in a teamwork way, so we will count you out for awhile. You may be *just a spectator*, a visitor in camp until you feel that you want to be one of us."

The boy walked away from the group somewhat downcast. When he returned to his full share of participation in the game some little time afterward, he came with a new spirit. He had learned something of the meaning of earning his opportunities of citizenship.

—*Walter MacPeek* in
GUIDANCE OF YOUTH

3

A Scout Is Helpful

He must be prepared at any time
... to save life,
... to help injured persons,
... and share the home duties.
He must do at least one
good turn to somebody
everyday.

An old French proverb says :"Mutual help is the law of nature," and another oft-quoted comment is, "When a friend asks, there is no tomorrow."

Of course our capacity to be helpful depends on our skill, our alertness to see the need of people around us, and our deep-seated capacity to care enough to help. A true Scout cares enough about mother and dad and teacher and leaders to do his share—plus.

Huber, the great naturalist, tells us that if a single

wasp discovers a deposit of honey or other food, he will return to his nest and impart the good news to his companions, who will sally forth in great numbers to partake of the fare which has been discovered for them.

> It's not what you'd do with a million
> If riches should e'er be your lot,
> But what you are doing at present
> With the dollar or quarter you've got.

RESPECT THE MAN WITH A BURDEN

George Washington and a friend were walking down a narrow street in Philadelphia when they met a laboring man carrying a heavy load on his shoulders. Washington stepped aside into the mud until the man had passed.

"Why did you allow yourself to be pushed off the walk?" asked his friend.

Washington explained that he was not "pushed off" but had given the other man the right-of-way. He said, "Look at his bent shoulders, and think of the hard work he does. One should always respect the man with a burden."

—W. D. Cavert in
WITH JESUS ON THE SCOUT TRAIL

UNTIL YOU POINTED IT OUT TO ME

An industrial leader in a Southern city some time ago presented a piece of land for a Scout camp to be named in honor of his old Scoutmaster.

"It is a very small way to show my appreciation for all he did for me," he said. "Once on an overnight trip we were camping on a hillside overlooking a beautiful valley. The night was soft and clear and all the stars were out.

"My old Scoutmaster pointed out and told me the names of numerous stars; told us of their immense distance and how they had been there for countless ages. He described the whole solar system. This simple story of the stars raised my personal horizon and gave me a new sense of reverence."

Another man said recently, "I never really saw a sunset until one evening my Scout leader pointed one out to me, calling my attention to the color and the beauty of it all. Since then, I've never looked at a sunset without seeing it with a new sense of wonder."

See what one man's influence can mean to others when he helps them see some of the not-always-obvious values around him?

—*Walter MacPeek*

A BILL FROM MOTHER

A boy's mother, a widow, found a note signed by her twelve-year-old son under her plate one morning. It read something like this, "Dear Mother—For carrying in six buckets of coal, twenty-five cents; making the fire four times, fifteen cents; going on two errands, ten cents. Total amount owed, fifty cents."

The mother rose from her chair, went to the dresser drawer, got her purse and took from it a half dollar which she put on the table near her boy's plate. The boy seemed highly pleased.

The next day, however, he discovered a note addressed to him under his plate at dinner time. It read, "Dear Willie—For providing food and clothing and a bed for twelve years, nothing. For dressing a baby boy for three years, nothing. For taking care of a boy with typhoid fever for eight weeks, nothing. For nursing an eight-year-old boy with scarlet fever for twelve weeks, nothing. Total, nothing."

Willie didn't look up for a long time. He was too busy thinking.

—Walter MacPeek

A SCOUTMASTER SAVES THE DAY

For weeks the troop had been engaged in expectant preparation for its parents' night program.

Everything was in order. The walls were filled with displays, the Scouts with enthusiasm, and the tables with good things to eat.

The toastmaster was well under way. The crowd sang with that restrained respectability which typifies a parents' night program.

Then Jimmie Davis rose to give his oration. This was the moment to which he had looked forward for many weeks. He caught a glimpse of the beaming face of his mother. He observed his father's stolid, assured countenance as he began. Jimmie started with a great burst of enthusiasm. He waxed more eloquent, conscious that his hearers were paying a high tribute to him by their careful attention.

Then something happened. The world seemed to swim before him. He slowed down—faltered—stopped. His face flushed and in desperation he looked toward his Scoutmaster.

Ever prepared, having heard that boyish masterpiece rehearsed again and again, the boy's leader supplied the missing words, and the boy went on. But somehow it was different now. The masterpiece had been marred.

Jimmie paused again, and again the Scoutmaster prompted him. And for the remaining two minutes the oration seemed more the Scoutmaster's than the boy's.

46

But Jimmie finished it. In the heart of the boy who sat down, knowing that he had failed, there was a heavy feeling. There was chagrin on his mother's face and his father's face indicated a pained consciousness of his son's failure.

The audience applauded in a perfunctory way, sorry for and pitying the boy whom they thought had failed.

But the Scoutmaster was on his feet. His quiet eyes shone. All listened quietly for his voice was low. What was he saying?

"I am more happy than any of you can possibly understand because of something that has just happened. You have seen a boy make a glorious victory out of what might have been a miserable failure.

"Jimmie had his chance to quit. To have quit would have been easy. But to finish the job, even in the face of two hundred people, required the highest kind of bravery and courage I know.

"Someday you may hear a better oratorical effect. But I am confident that you will never see a finer demonstration of the spirit of our troop—to play the game even under difficulties—than Jimmie has just given you."

The people thundered their applause now. Jimmie's mother sat straight and proud. The old look of assurance was back on the face of Jimmie's father. The entire group was enthusiastic again. And Jimmie, with a lump in his throat, said something to the Scout beside him that sounded like, "Gee, if I can ever be that kind of Scoutmaster."

—Walter MacPeek

UNHERALDED AND UNSUNG

You know that the very heart of Scouting is tied up with the practical concept of our living as good citizens. Every Scout is taught to do his full share to help in matters of common good and to be cooperative and helpful to people around him.

The real Scout *lives* his code. This spirit of helpfulness—even at considerable cost to himself—reaches its highest level each year in more than three hundred incidents of meritorious service and heroism in which a Cub Scout, Boy Scout, or Explorer goes far beyond the call of duty to be helpful in an emergency.

Some of these boys risk their lives; others give their lives in helping in situations in saving or attempting to save life.

These dramatic incidents are important. They inspire us.

Yet your good turns and the day-after-day good turns of millions of Scouts everywhere—unheralded

48

and unknown—also add up to truly significant and far-reaching influence.

HE DIDN'T FORGET

E. F. Pierson, Kansas City industrialist, has no sons of his own but he shows his concern for other men's sons in a most far-reaching way. In 1961 he sponsored a class of 452 Eagle Scouts. They were outstanding boys from all parts of the far-flung Kansas City Area Council, which serves a large segment of the state—boys in some eleven counties.

"I want to see that every one of these boys who wants to go to college has his chance to go," Mr. Pierson said.

But he didn't stop with hoping. He employed a high school counselor to interview each of the 452 boys and inaugurated a file of information about each of them.

His program was based on the facts that of all the graduating high school students in the United States only about 23 percent go on to college, and of all the graduating high school students in the greater Kansas City area only about 30 percent continue their education.

These were disturbing figures to Mr. Pierson, for he realized that competition and the need for more special skills are increasing, not only in our own country but in the whole world, and that the continuance of the United States as a powerful influence in the world depends now, more than ever, on the education of its people.

He called this program "Operation Research" and carried it through to show how these averages might be raised through special counseling of a cross section of students in the greater Kansas City area.

He wrote the 452 Eagle Scouts, "You, as a member of the E. F. Pierson Eagle Scout class, have been selected to take part in this important project.

"A primary purpose of Operation Research is to assist you in developing into a valuable citizen no matter what field you choose as a lifetime pursuit.

"The special services of Operation Research will be made available to you. If qualified, you may be assisted in receiving funds from one of the many grants and scholarships provided for students in this area.

"Of course, you will carry the greatest load by making yourself worthy of the assistance that Operation Research can help you obtain."

A reunion of the Pierson class of Eagle Scouts was held in 1962 at Pierson Hall at the University of Missouri and others in 1963 and in 1964. More than 80 percent of the boys of the class are now in college. Some are in the armed services.

The entire outcome of Operation Research can never be fully known. How many boys' lives will be entirely different because of this one man's efforts will never be known. The result of one man's encouragement can never be measured.

A man had an idea and he put it to work. He looked into the promises written on the faces of 452 outstanding boys. And he didn't forget.

—Walter MacPeek

THE MERIT BADGE COUNSELOR

A merit badge counselor looked quizzically at a Scout. "Woodcarving, eh?" he observed. "And this is made from a peach pit? Carved it with your pocket knife? It's a neat piece of work."

And then the kindly counselor went on to point out that the Scout had not really used the tools of a wood-carver—that excellent as this peach stone neckerchief slide was, the Scout had not fully met the requirements for the merit badge.

"But now that you have this good start, how would you like to go ahead and meet all the requirements and come back to see me again in a few weeks?"

The Scout came back three weeks later and brought a beautifully carved bas-relief of Old Ironsides—a piece of artistic workmanship of which both he and the counselor were proud.

And so the Scout had one more experience in doing a task thoroughly and completely.

Wouldn't it have been a tragedy if the merit badge counselor had worked on a good-enough-to-get-by philosophy and had permitted the Scout to defeat his chance to do the job right? It's worth thinking about. —*Walter MacPeek*

HE KNEW HOW

In Troop 456, made up of rural boys centering around Pond, Missouri, many of the Scouts come five, six, or even eight miles to attend troop meetings.

One evening after Scoutmaster Roscoe Oxford had demonstrated artificial respiration to the Scouts of the troop, each Scout practiced on another Scout. Part of the Scout code is to be prepared, as you well know.

Nine days later, a few miles from the troop meeting place, lightning struck the barn in which Scout Daniel Lee Johnson, thirteen, together with his father, brother, and sister, had taken refuge from the rain. The bolt struck Daniel's brother and sister, burning them and knocking them to the floor.

Daniel—with his nine days' knowledge of artificial respiration—didn't hesitate a moment, but started to work, instructing his father to do the same. Soon, both brother and sister were breathing again.

The doctor, called to treat the children, said that the prompt use of artificial respiration had "unquestionably saved their lives." A certificate of merit was awarded Scout Johnson.

A tragedy was averted because, nine days before, a Scout had learned artificial respiration well enough to put it to use.

THE ROAD AHEAD

Fellows, I'm not going to tell you who I'm talking about. And I'm sure this Scout won't mind my telling you what we said to each other.

We had a good visit together—this Scout and I— one evening last week, and I've been thinking every once in a while since then about our discussion.

"I'm afraid there won't be anything really important left for me to do," he told me, adding, "Lincoln and Lindbergh and Edison and Byrd and those people have got everything pretty much discovered and invented already. I'm 'fraid there won't be anything left but routine jobs when I am grown. I wish I had been born a hundred years ago."

I see some of you fellows smiling.

Well, I smiled, too and I told him, "Son, about twenty-five years ago I felt this same way about things. But somehow our old world has kept right on blazing new trails and traveling into new fields, even more than in any previous quarter of a century in all history. You need not worry very much about there not being big enough jobs for you. Better spend your time gettin' ready so that you'll be big enough for the job that comes along."

He agreed with me, and I think you will, too.

—*Walter MacPeek*

4

A Scout Is Friendly

He is a friend to all
... and a brother
... to every other Scout.

What a cold, dark world this would be if we had no friends—no one to look to us with friendly smile and happy recognition.

Gray, in "Elegy Written in a Country Churchyard," wrote, "He gained from Heaven ('twas all he wished) a friend."

Friend of my bosom, thou art more than a brother, why wert thou not born in my father's dwelling?
—*Charles Lamb*

"Those friends thou hast," the immortal Shakespeare wrote, "grapple them to thy soul with hoops of steel."

Emerson attributes to Omar Khayyam, "He who has a thousand friends has not a friend to spare,

And he who has one enemy will meet him everywhere.

> It is my joy in life to find
>   At every turning of the road,
> The strong arm of a comrade kind
>   To help me onward with my load.
>
> And since I have no gold to give,
>   And love alone must make amends,
> My only prayer is, while I live—
>   God make me worthy of my friends!
>   —Frank Dempster Sherman
>   "A Prayer"

FALSE RUMOR

Some of you mathematicians might want to check up on this one. I haven't figured it out, but I have it on good authority that if two persons, after exchanging a false rumor, each told his rumor to two more people within fifteen minutes and then those four people, on hearing it, would pass it on to each of two more within fifteen minutes, and this process kept going, that soon the number would reach that of the population of the United States.

How long do you think it would take theoretically for this to happen? We might try to guess.

We won't keep you in suspense. The answer is that in less than six hours and forty-five minutes the rumor would make the rounds of our entire country.

There is a moral to this little announcement, but I know that it's not necessary to tell you what it is.

NEW COURAGE

The college president happened to be walking across the campus with the young man. They were leaving the graduating class banquet.

"Boy," he said, putting his hand on the boy's shoulders, "I've always liked you. I've always believed in you. You have great possibilities. I know I am going to have the chance to be proud of you someday. You've got it in you."

Now what do you imagine that did for that young man? It nerved him against future discouragements. It came back to him again and again when the going was tough. It built him up and made future accomplishment almost a "must."

I know. You see, I was that boy.

—*Norman Vincent Peale* in THE POWER OF
POSITIVE THINKING FOR YOUNG PEOPLE

THOUGHTFULNESS AND UNDERSTANDING

It's strange, isn't it, the things that stand out most vividly in our memories. A young man in Detroit told me of an experience he had years ago.

"I'll always remember that night," he said. "Uncle Otto (Hornung) was talking. Everybody was listening hard because we all love Uncle Otto. Besides he always says something.

"I was trying to take a picture and my flashbulb exploded and made a terrific noise like a gun shot. Uncle Otto paused a moment and then went right on. I felt awful, so embarrassed I wanted to run.

"But after Uncle Otto had finished speaking he came across the room, put his hand on my shoulder, and said, 'It's O. K., Son. Things like that happen sometimes.' Boy, did I feel better!"

—*Walter MacPeek*

A NICKNAME REPLACED

Everybody laughed at George. Years ago they had nicknamed him "Bum"—a rather natural nickname for him. At first he had resented the nickname in his boyish way, but now he was hardened to it. He had learned to "take it."

George was fat and awkward and gave people the impression that he was lazy. He grabbed for his food and swallowed it half chewed, and altogether his table manners at camp weren't much to boast about. When boys laughed at him—with boyish sense of humor always greater than their sense of respect—he pretended not to care. When people made fun of him, his feelings were hurt but he didn't know how to change things, so he feigned indifference.

He had become a Scout and he liked his Patrol Leader. He was proud of his Tenderfoot badge, but his folks at home didn't seem to care much whether he was a Scout or not.

One day last summer a leader at Scout camp began calling George "Happy." A new feeling came up inside of George. Here was someone who didn't call him "Bum."

That new nickname seemed to catch on. Of course, George didn't know that the camp leader had talked the situation over with the gang and they had plotted together to give him a better nickname to live up to.

"Hap" finally became the accepted name for the roly-poly boy, and "Bum" was forgotten. And along with the change of nickname came a change *inside* the boy. After all, a fellow has to live up to what folks expect of him—especially the gang in the Scout Troop.

"Hap" often repeats the words of the Scout Law now, and he's trying hard to live up to them all.

But somehow the fourth, "A Scout Is Friendly," and the eighth, "A Scout Is Cheerful," seem to be his own personal property. —*Walter MacPeek*

OUT PLAYING

"What's Jim doing, Edna?"

"Nothing—he's out playing," the boy's mother replied as she looked across the room at her husband.

It was true that Jimmie Edmunds was out playing. But in saying that he was doing nothing his mother had unintentionally made one of the gravest misstatements of her life.

At that moment Jim was making a decision—meeting one of those frequent and far-reaching crises of boyhood.

"I'll punch your nose if you don't let him alone. He's littler than you," Jimmie was saying in a voice not exactly carefully modulated.

"Oh, yeah?"

"I guess you heard me. You let him alone. Go on home, Billy. I'll see that you're safe." All the while clenched fists gesticulated and pairs of defiant eyes glared into each other. The aggressor sniffed and walked on up the street. Evidently there was to be no bloodshed.

"Thanks, Jim, you're a peach. You didn't need to run the chance just to protect me."

"Chance? That wasn't no chance. I could lick him with one finger."

"Sure you could. But just the same, it'd a been rough on me if you hadn't jumped in."

"That's nothin'. Nothin' a'tall! You'll know just how easy it is when you're as big as me."

Jimmie whistled as he ambled down the street. He felt quite a thrill of satisfaction down inside. He was glad that he had stepped in to protect a small boy from a bully. His shoulders were thrown back as he slammed the door, flung his cap halfway across the room and successfully caught it on a hook.

"What have you been doing, Jimmie?" his mother asked.

"Nothin'. Just playin'," her son replied.

"You're surely growing, Son," the boy's father observed as he looked up from his paper.

"Yeah," Jimmie replied, and then added, "guess I am," as he thought of the episode of ten minutes ago.

And the father never knew how nearly he had hit the nail on the head.　　　　　—M. Retlaw

RESULTS REACHED FAR

A group of sullen, disconsolate German prisoners of war were being marched ashore at Plymouth, England, during World War II. One in particular, hardly more than a boy, looked so utterly discouraged and forlorn that a King's Scout (Eagle Scout to you) who was watching was moved to give him a warm, friendly smile. To his surprise the German prisoner's face lighted up and he responded with the Scout salute, recognizing the uniform the English Scout was wearing. The King Scout fell into step beside the German boy, chatting with him as long as the authorities permitted it.

At the World Jamboree in Bad Ischl, Austria, one of the Section Chiefs, relating the incident, commented, "That simple act of Scout friendliness was the thing which aroused in the heart of that half-sick, dejected, defeated German soldier the determination to stick it out and to continue in scouting when release came. I know, for I was that German soldier." —SCOUTING

WORTH TRYING

"Baden-Powell, whose identity was unknown to the boys, once asked a group what they were playing," Goeffrey Bond tells in *The Baden-Powell Story*.

"Every voice now took up the explanation in a different way so that Baden-Powell finally had to wave them into an unwilling silence," Bond tells. They were playing Boers and soldiers, reliving BP's exploits at the siege of Mafeking. "Well, don't let me stop your game. It sounds like good fun," BP told the boys.

"Oh, you'd love it, mister," echoed the boys as he turned to go, and one threw the parting remark after him, "You ought to try it sometime."

FRIENDSHIP SHOWN TO A BOY

The following incident, centering around the boyhood days of W. Ben Hunt, famous Indian lore expert, handicrafter, and wood-carver, reveals something of how our mind works.

When Ben was a boy of twelve, a band of Sioux Indians came to Milwaukee with the Buffalo Bill Wild West Show, the first Indians whom Ben had ever seen. They fascinated him with their buckskin leggins, their war bonnets of eagle feathers, and their painted faces. Several were famous warriors who had helped defeat Custer at the Little Big Horn.

Young Ben Hunt hung around their tepees all day trying to talk to them, but they completely ignored the bashful boy.

"If there were only some way I could figure out how to get them to notice me. If I could only think of something they want, maybe I could get them to talk," Ben thought.

Then he remembered the wild rabbits in back of

the park. Gathering up his courage he hinted to one of the Indians that he might like some wild meat for a change. It wasn't very long until the twelve-year-old Milwaukee boy was talking cottontails with a band of the wildest Indians that ever came off the Western plains.

After the hunt the Indians took Ben back to their encampment and invited him into their tepees. They skinned the rabbits and threw them into cooking pots for their dinner while the fascinated boy watched. Soon the circus band started to play and it was time for the big show to begin. The old chief put his arm around Ben's shoulder and said, "Come." He led the boy right through the performer's entrance into the Big Top where he was their guest for the show.

"I was the envy of all the kids in Milwaukee that day when they saw how friendly those Indians were to me. Never again did I have to pay to get into a Buffalo Bill Wild West Show."

From that interest shown in a boy by a group of circus Indians, an interest in Indian lore developed until today this famous artist and writer for *Boys' Life* and author of numerous books is one of the leading authorities on Indian lore in the country.

The dividends that come from friendliness can sometimes reach far.   —Walter MacPeek

THEY WERE HIS FRIENDS

"Yes, I have three friends in America—Benjamin Franklin, Abraham Lincoln, and Harriet Beecher Stowe," said Michael Pupin, a Serbian boy, when he first landed at Ellis Island and the immigration officers asked him if he had any friends in this country. Michael had only five cents in his pocket, and it was against the rules to admit a person unless he had money enough to support himself until he found a steady job. But the officers decided that any boy would make a good citizen if he had read so much about these three great Americans that he considered them his friends. So he was admitted and became one of our leading inventors.

—*W. D. Cavert* in WITH JESUS
ON THE SCOUT TRAIL

MAGIC ROPE

I picked some scraps of rope apart
To see how they were made.
Most of it was twisted hemp
Yet some was cotton braid.

And from the stuff I played with
I thought aloud: "Rope size runs
To hawsers that hold battleships
of fifty thousand tons."

But there's another kind of rope
Not made by a machine
Stronger than the best steel cable.
Yet so fine it can't be seen.

I'm not talking of the kind of rope
That anybody buys
But the magic line of friendship
That holds two friendly guys.

I learned a lot of things at camp
But the best trick that I got
Was to take that line of friendship
And tie the proper knot.
—David H. McKenzie
in Scouting

OLD FRIENDSHIPS RECALLED

I've been trying to write an editorial. It's pretty poor stuff as editorials go, yet it might have done if I had finished it. Now it lies in my wastebasket, unfinished, torn across the middle.

It was to have been an arousing article on "Friendships—Our Richest Possessions." It was to tell of the stimulation and enrichment that can come to us from association with true friends. It was to touch the heart of those who read it, to aid them perhaps in recalling some acquaintance whose friendship had been life-changing.

But somehow as I wrote word after word my pen

faltered. I became conscious that my mind was wandering—that I too was in a state of reminiscence. Somewhere out in the state of Washington my thoughts were traveling to an old friend of mine, one who inspired and strengthened my life more than he will ever know—one whose life had been a sort of pattern for my own.

"I must write to him sometime," I told myself, then forced myself to turn back to my editorial on "Friendships."

A few more words and my mind was again traveling, this time somewhere into Canada. I haven't heard from "Uncle" Jim for a year or two. We called him "Uncle" because he was more sober and sedate than the rest of the gang. There flashed before my eyes the vivid pictured recollection of Jim Barnes around the campfire—But I must finish this editorial.

Then, as I tried to add more straggling words, I recalled an old teacher. Somehow in those days of turbulent adolescence she had seen clear through the make-believe of boyish bravado into the heart of a groping boy. She had understood. What has become of her in these many years? Perhaps she is married now with sons of her own.

I think back to Phil and his sense of integrity, his fairness, his love of people. That was years ago. He is now our Ambassador to Greece.

A few more labored sentences added to the manuscript before me, and then I become conscious that I am sharing the burden of my old roommate, now a clergyman in a little midwestern town. Dick—a preacher! It hardly seems possible. Well, Dick will make things happen right—wherever he is. His concern for people and his sense of teamwork with God will make a difference in the lives of people.

Then I pictured an airplane and its pilot, handsome and boyish in his enthusiasm—ever ready for a daring challenge. A lesser Lindbergh. Only a few years ago he was a promising boy. I know the kind of man he must be now.

And as the recollections and reminiscence spin on and on, I am in sunny California, in rugged old New Hampshire, way down near the Rio Grande, across the sea to England, and on into Germany. Memories of neglected, almost forgotten friendships —rarest and most priceless of all possessions—crowd in upon me.

The worthless manuscript before me becomes a crumpled scrap of paper. A dominating purpose grips me. I am going to write some letters.

—Walter MacPeek

5

A Scout Is Courteous

He is polite to all,
... especially to women,
... and children,
... old people,
... and the weak and helpless.
He must not take pay
... for being helpful
... or courteous.

John Billings wrote: "No man shall beat me in politeness, not so long as politeness continues to be as cheap as it is now."

Courtesy does not require additional time. It is merely a pleasant attitude of heart which helps to sweeten life as we travel along day after day.

Courtesy isn't something extra—it can be a part of everything we do. Someone has defined courtesy as the air in the tires that takes most of the jolts out of our ride through life!

It is not a slam at you when people are rude. It is a slam at the people they have met before.

—*F. Scott Fitzgerald*

COURTESY IN ACTION

More than two thousand years ago an old man went to the Olympic games in Greece. He was late. The marble benches were filled with thousands of people. Not a single seat was empty.

A Spartan youth, seeing the old man's plight, gave him his seat. A group of young Athenians, observing the incident, applauded.

The old man turned to them and said, "You Athenians *know* what is right to do. The Spartans *do* it."

TRADITIONS AND VALUES

More than thirty years ago I knew the leaders and boys of Troop 8, Washington, D.C., and came to have high respect for this troop.

When they invited me to speak at their forty-fifth anniversary reunion I accepted with pleasure—for several reasons. This would be an opportunity to pay a tribute to a really great Scoutmaster who had died two years ago. I was pretty sure that this would be a well-planned occasion with the spotlight on boys with parents genuinely proud and truly sharing in the troop progress.

Yet I couldn't help wondering as I went to the meeting would things be the same? Would the values of courtesy and thoughtfulness and good taste still stand out as they did in those days of thirty years ago? I recalled how someone had once said that Troop 8's boys were outstanding campers and all-around good Scouts, but that their specialty was being thoughtful gentlemen.

On the night of the reunion I had hardly stepped inside the room until a Scout extended his hand, told me his name, smiled and said, "We're glad you are going to be with us tonight." A few minutes later another Scout introduced himself and welcomed me. And before the dinner started, most of the boys of the troop welcomed me in this way. I knew, of course, that things like this don't "just happen." They are a result of training.

I was satisfied then that the spirit of old Troop 8 had not lessened. I knew that wise leaders were continuing to emphasize the everyday practice of courtesy and thoughtfulness.

Traditions live on and genuine values, once emphasized, continue to be important.

—Walter MacPeek

A HEAD-ON COLLISION

Of course it takes time to be polite, and somehow we seem to be in a terrific hurry these days. But if we are on guard we can even be polite without slowing up a bit. Brown was in a hurry—had to meet a friend at the station in just seven minutes. Grabbing his hat he tore out the door and down the side street at a two-forty gait. White had stopped to visit just three minutes too long and simply had to get to a certain place before the clock struck the hour. At the corner Brown and White collided head on. White flared up in a second. What earthly right had any other human being getting in *his* way? In an instant his fist was doubled up and Brown was about to get the sound thrashing that he deserved, *but Brown was smiling.* White could hardly believe his eyes, but it was true.

"My dear sir," said Brown in a cherry, friendly voice, "I don't know whether you bumped into me or whether I bumped into you, but if I ran into you, I beg your pardon. If you bumped into me, don't mention it. So long, see you later," and Brown was off toward the station.

It was Emerson who warned us that "life is not so short but what there is always time for courtesy."

—*F. H. Chelsy* in

THE PRACTICE OF THE OATH AND LAW

ONE BOY IN FIFTY

A gentleman advertised for a boy to assist him in his office, and nearly fifty applicants presented themselves. Out of the whole number he selected one and dismissed the rest.

"I should like to know," said a friend, "on what ground you selected that boy, who had not a single recommendation."

"You are mistaken," said the gentleman. "He had a great many. He wiped his feet when he came in and closed the door after him, showing that he was careful. He gave his seat instantly to that lame old man, showing that he was kind and thoughtful.

"He took off his cap when he came in, and answered my questions promptly, showing that he was polite and gentlemanly. He picked up the book which I had purposely laid on the floor, and replaced it upon the table, while all the rest stepped over it, showing that he was orderly; and he waited quietly for his turn, instead of pushing and crowding. When I talked to him, I noticed that his clothing was tidy, his hair neatly brushed, and his fingernails clean."

—TRUE STORIES OF REAL SCOUTS

A COURTEOUS DISTINCTION

In 1784 Jefferson was named by Congress minister to France in place of Benjamin Franklin, who, after long and remarkable service there, had begged leave to come home. Then it was that the Virginian made his kind and courteous acknowledgment of the greatness of his famous colleague and associate of the "Declaration" days.

"You replace Dr. Franklin, I hear," said the Prime Minister of King Louis of France when Mr. Jefferson was introduced to him at the court.

Jefferson bowed with his customary dignity and courtesy. "Sir," he said, "I succeed Dr. Franklin; no one can replace him." —Target

SELF-CONTROL

When Henry Clay Trumball was a young man, a superior in the engineer's office where he was at work rebuked him for taking from the former's desk a special ink bottle. "Don't let this happen again," the man said.

A few days later the ink was again missing. "Henry, bring me the ink," the man called. Henry obeyed, though he found the ink on the desk of another clerk. Then he took the scolding that followed.

Later the clerk at fault told that he, not Henry, was to blame. "Why didn't you tell me, Henry?" asked his superior. "You didn't ask me, Sir," was the quiet reply. This evidence of self-control was not lost on the questioner; he knew that it would tell in the clerk's later life.   —*John T. Faris*

THOUGHTFUL SCOUT

At one of the Jamboree Trading Posts a Scout had spread out an attractive display of "swapping stock," including some fine neckerchief silks, badges, and beadwork. At the nearby snack bar, a lady, picking up her cup of coffee, found it too hot to handle, juggled it desperately for a moment, and lost control of it. As it fell it drenched the Scout's prized collection of beautiful souvenirs. But there was no word of angry protest—not even a rueful glance at the thoroughly ruined display. Instead, this real Scout was instantly on his feet, inquiring anxiously of the startled and dismayed lady, "Ma'am, did you burn yourself?"   —Scouting

6

A Scout Is Kind

He is a friend to animals.
He will not kill or hurt
... any living creature needlessly,
... but will strive to save,
... and protect all harmless life.

He is thoughtful about being kind and alert to find opportunities to show kindness and consideration.

The unknown author of "My Daily Creed" wrote:

Let me be a little kinder,
Let me be a little blinder
To the faults of those around me.

Henry Burton, in "Pass It On" wrote:

Have you had a kindness shown?
Pass it on.

'Twas not given for thee alone,
    Pass it on.
Let it travel down the years,
    Let it wipe another's tears,
'Till in heav'n the deed appears—
    Pass it on.

Emily Dickinson summed up the essence of kindness when she wrote:

If I can stop one heart from breaking,
I shall not live in vain;
If I can ease one life the aching,
Or cool one pain,
Or help one fainting robin
Unto his nest again,
I shall not live in vain.

GREAT-HEARTED LINCOLN

Lincoln's sympathies went forth to animals as well as to his fellowmen. On one of his visits to General Grant's headquarters during the Civil War, his attention was attracted to three tiny kittens crawling about the floor. The mother had died, and the little wanderers in their grief were mewing piteously.

Mr. Lincoln picked them up tenderly, sat down on a camp chair, took them on his knees, stroked their soft fur, and murmured, "Poor little creatures! Don't cry! You'll be taken good care of." Then, turning to an officer, he said, "Colonel, I hope you will see that these poor little motherless waifs are given plenty of good milk and treated kindly."

Three times the President went to that tent during his short visit and picked up those little kittens, fondled them as they lay on his knee, purring their gratitude. It seemed a strange sight, on the eve of battle when everyone was thinking only of the science of destruction, to see the hand that by a stroke of the pen had loosed the shackles of four million bondmen, and had signed the commission of every officer of that gallant army, from the general-in-chief to the humblest lieutenant, tenderly caressing three stray kittens.

—Our Dumb Animals

TOMMY MEETS A CRISIS

You may laugh at this story. Then again, maybe the picture of Tommy in action will touch something down inside you that will make a lump come into your throat. It's a yarn about an ordinary boy —just a nine-year-old Cub Scout who faced a crisis —and came through.

Tommy had a keen eye. Boylike, he didn't look very long at any one thing for fear he might miss something up ahead. At the same time his sharp eye didn't miss much that went on near him. One day he noticed a low-hanging bird's nest in a tree in his backyard. As the days went by, he watched the nest and soon discovered that it housed a mother bird and five tiny ones, too young to fly.

It was hard to keep himself back, but Tommy watched from a distance, realizing that the bird might interpret his presence as an intrusion if he came too close. Birds don't quite trust grown-ups— or boys either.

But one day Tommy sensed tragedy. Something was wrong with the mother bird. Tommy got up close, just as quietly as he could, talked in a low tone to the bird, and sized up the situation. The mother bird was injured; she couldn't get up into the nest, only a foot or two above Tommy's head.

This was a crisis to the mother bird—and to Cub Scout Tommy. He had been trained to care and to help. He realized that if the mother bird couldn't get to her nest that the five little ones would die.

There may be some grown-ups who might have shrugged their shoulders and, muttering something about being "too busy," merely felt sorry for the birds. But Tommy was nine years old and a Cub Scout—he *had* to do something.

So, tenderly, eagerly, he came close to the fluttering bird. He spread his fingers underneath the injured mother bird and helped her to her nest. He saw that one wing was broken. As he placed her carefully into her nest the chirping of the hungry baby birds quieted down.

As the weeks went by, no white-robed nurse in any stately hospital cared more earnestly for her charges than did Tommy. He dug worms. He brought food from the kitchen. Each time he carefully lifted the mother bird into and out of the nest. Finally the broken wing healed. The mother bird could find food for her young now and she began to teach them to fly.

And nine-year-old Cub Scout Tommy is supremely happy. He saved six lives.

—*Walter MacPeek*

ABRAHAM LINCOLN'S KINDNESS

In the early pioneer days, when Abraham Lincoln was a young lawyer and "rode the circuit," he was one day traveling on horseback from one town to another with a party of friends who were lawyers like himself.

The road which they traveled led across prairies and through woods. As they passed by a grove where the birds were singing merrily, they noticed a young bird which had fallen from the nest and lay fluttering by the roadside. After they had gone a short distance, Mr. Lincoln stopped, turned, and said, "Wait for me a moment. I will soon rejoin you."

As his friends halted and watched him, they saw Mr. Lincoln return to the place where the helpless bird lay on the ground and tenderly take it up and set it on a limb near the nest.

When he joined his companions, one of them laughingly asked, "Why did you bother yourself and delay us with such a trifle as that?"

Abraham Lincoln's reply deserves to be remembered. "My friend," said he, "I can only say this— that I feel better for it. I could not have slept tonight if I had left that helpless little creature to perish on the ground."

—Our Dumb Animals

MAN'S BEST FRIEND

The Scout talked so enthusiastically about the good time he had at camp that his parents were a little disappointed that he hadn't missed home.

"Weren't you at all anxious to get home?" his father asked.

"Well," replied the boy, thoughtfully, "not specially." He paused for a minute, and then added, "Some of the fellows were—those that had dogs."

—from Troop 20, Yakima, Washington

81

GREAT-HEARTED

Garibaldi was the leader of an army fighting for a free and united Italy. He was camping near a mountain when a shepherd came in the early evening and asked for help in finding a lamb which had been lost. Garibaldi ordered a band of men to form a searching party. Taking lanterns, they hunted several hours without success. Finally they returned to their tents and went to bed, but their leader did not give up so easily. The next morning when the orderly went to the general's tent, he was surprised at what he saw. Garibaldi was asleep with the lost lamb in his arms. Imagine a great general, engaged in a war for freedom, being so tenderhearted that he spent the night finding a lamb! Busy as he was, he was willing to take time for kindness.

—W. D. Cavert in WITH JESUS
ON THE SCOUT TRAIL

A DOG AND A PORCUPINE

At a northern summer colony a dog "tenderfoot" had gaily tackled a porcupine. He was speeding madly for home, a flying pincushion, and telling the world about it. His mistress sprang to meet him and attempted to withdraw the barbed quills.

In his fright the suffering animal turned on the woman and bit her. She tried again, in vain. Then she sent to a nearby Scout camp for help. The boys responded on the run. Gathering round the dog two of them endeavored to hold him while a third sought to draw one of the quills. The animal fought them, yelping and snapping viciously.

"It's no use. Take him to the doctor," she said.

The boys made fast time to the resort doctor. In his office the physician administered chloroform and proceeded to extract the quills.

The last quill was withdrawn. The kneeling Scouts patted and spoke to the dog. It continued to lie flat and inert. Finally the doctor shook his head sadly. "I'm afraid he's gone," he said. "I am not used to giving animals chloroform. I must have given him too much."

The Scouts were not ready to accept the verdict. Carrying the limp animal outdoors, they stretched it on the ground as though it were a human and began giving it artificial respiration. In a few minutes the dog's ears twitched. Its eyes opened, it looked about. Suddenly it leaped to its feet, barked and ran and jumped into the boat—ready for the trip home with its Scout friends.   —BOYS' LIFE

VACATION TRAIN WRECKED

It was a wholesale sixth point-of-the-Law opportunity that came the way of Scout Jack Baldwin.

With his parents he was bound north on a "Summer Vacation Special" that was carrying numerous family parties to their summer places in the lake country of Quebec. In the baggage car were the family cats and dogs.

Nearing the little town of Bic the train suddenly left the rails. Although it was fortunately not traveling fast, several coaches were thrown on their sides in the ditch.

As soon as he found himself and his parents unhurt, Jack began helping other passengers who needed assistance. Then he thought of the animals.

He scrambled from the coach and ran forward. As he feared, the baggage car also was in the ditch, on its side; and within was a promiscuous pile of trunks, valises, boxes, and crates containing the trapped animals.

Jack lowered himself inside and, speaking quietly and reassuringly, first freed the leashed dogs, who quickly scrambled to the door and jumped out. The conductor and baggageman then appeared, and with them Jack began freeing the other animals. The anxious owners gathered outside, and as the animals were released, they were passed out. It proved a full two-hours' job, and sometimes was ticklish work, dodging a pair of suddenly snapping jaws or the quick lunge of a panicky cat. But careful, quiet work and soothing talk did it.

Afterwards Jack amused himself wondering just how many times that day he had carried out the sixth point of the Law by being kind to "an animal."

—*Frank E. L. Coombs* in
Boys' LIFE

HORSE THROUGH THE ICE

During the north country winter, farmers often use shortcuts to town across frozen lakes and streams and on dark nights carry lanterns on their sleighs. Occasionally sleighs break through the ice, and occupants and horses are drowned. One winter's night Lone Scout Ralph Brown, whose home overlooked one of the small lakes of eastern Ontario, was called by his mother to see a lantern light out on the lake. "It hasn't moved for some time," she said. "Perhaps someone's in trouble."

As Ralph dashed out on the lake he called. A man's voice replied, "I've broken through! I can't get out of the cutter!"

At the scene Ralph found a black circle of broken ice and water, in the center a man's figure on the top of the sleigh seat, and a horse in water up to his back.

"I'll get my dad and our boat," Ralph cried, and sped back shoreward. Dragging the boat to the hole, they rowed to the cutter and rescued the farmer.

"No hope for the horse," the farmer said, "even if we could get him loose."

Ralph had another idea. He whipped out his Scout knife and cut the boat's rope painter. He tied it about his waist and gave the end to his father. He worked the bow of the boat to the side of the horse, leaned over, head down under the water beneath the animal, and cut the traces. The horse struggled free of the cutter shafts, and finally they succeeded in dragging him ashore. There Ralph took care of the trembling animal with a good rubdown and blankets, in the stable, while his father and mother looked after the farmer.

—BOYS' LIFE

7

A Scout Is Obedient

He obeys his parents,
...Scoutmaster, Patrol Leader,
...and all other
duly constituted authorities.

What would happen if an engineer did not obey signals? What would be the result if all people ignored stop lights on the street and highway? "Obedience to law is liberty," someone has said.

And, of course, the most important obedience of all is that obedience to the highest law—that which we know in our hearts to be God's wish.

True obedience is true liberty.
—*Henry Ward Beecher*

Obedience alone gives the right to command.
—*Emerson*

Obey a man with cordial loyalty and you will understand him. —*Phillips Brooks*

87

I find the doing of the will of God leaves me no
time for disputing about his plans.

—*George MacDonald*

REPENTANT FOR DISOBEDIENCE

Samuel Johnson, one of the best-known writers in
England during a former century, was one day seen
standing with bare head before a shop in which his
father once sold books. People wondered what he
was doing. Afterward he told his friends he was
trying to make up for disobeying his father fifty
years before. Johnson's father was ill and asked his
son to take charge of the shop. The boy refused to
go. He was a proud young man and did not like to
do the work of a shopkeeper. After his father's death
he was ashamed of his disobedience and wanted to
do something to show how sorry he was.

—*W. D. Cavert* in WITH JESUS ON
THE SCOUT TRAIL

HOW STONEWALL GOT HIS NAME

General Stonewall Jackson, when at West Point
was deficient in his studies, but while he obediently
put out his lights at "Taps" he piled his grate with
coal, and by the firelight, studied late into the night.
He compiled for his own use a set of rules and
maxims. Characteristic ones are: "Through life let

your principal object be the discharge of duty."
"Sacrifice your life rather than your word."

For his devoted gallantry in the battle of Chapulte-
pec, he was made brevet major. When asked later
why he did not run when his commander was disabled, his characteristic reply was, "I was not ordered
to do so. I was ordered to hold my position, and I
had no right to abandon it."

In after years he confessed that the part he played
in stepping out and assuring his men that there was
no danger when a cannon ball passed between his
legs was the only wilful falsehood he ever told in his
life. At Manassas Junction, when the South Carolina
troops were overwhelmed, Jackson's brigade saved
the day and General Lee cried to his men, "Look
at Jackson. There he stands like a stone wall. Rally
behind the Virginian." This was the origin of the
sobriquet, "Stonewall" by which he is known in
history.   —*James Terry White*

UNDAUNTED BY WELLINGTON

An English boy was once set to watch his father's
field. On no account was he to let anyone go through
it. The boy had scarcely taken his post when some
huntsmen came up and ordered him to open the
gate. He declined to do so, telling them that he
meant to obey his orders.

At last one of them came up and said in commanding tones: "My boy, you do not know me, but I am the Duke of Wellington. I am not accustomed to being disobeyed. I command you to open the gate."

The boy lifted his cap and answered firmly, "I am sure the Duke of Wellington would not wish me to obey his orders. I must keep the gate shut. No one can pass through but by my master's express permission."

Then the duke took off his own hat and said, "I honor the man or boy who can neither be frightened nor bribed into disobeying orders. With an army of such soldiers I could conquer not only the French, but the world." —Young Folks' Treasury

CHAMPION ROPE SPLICER

Breakfast was over and the camp director stood in front of the mess hall making a short talk. He cleared his throat and launched into his announcement.

"Scouts, there is a very brave camper among us. He was so brave that in the dark of the night he went down behind all the tents last night and cut the ropes that had been placed there for airing our blankets and clothes. This very brave camper, if he's as brave as I think he is, is going to come to me immediately after breakfast, and he is going to have a busy day."

You could have heard a pin drop throughout the mess hall. Everybody was quiet. It was a painful quietness.

"I'm afraid he isn't going to be trampled down by boys coming up and telling him they were the guilty one," I said to myself as I stood back in an alcove and waited.

But sure enough, a moment later a tousled-haired youngster approached the camp director and shuffling his feet, with a guilty grin indicating that he wasn't exactly comfortable in his present role, looked into the camp director's face and said, "Well, when do I begin splicing the ropes?"

The boy who had made a mistake spliced rope all day long. By nightfall he was the champion rope splicer of the whole camp. But even more than that, he had won the full admiration of every man and boy in the camp. He had made good in a tough spot.

He had made a mistake. He had made a mess of things, yet he was man enough to admit his failure, admit his mistake, and do what he could to correct it. —*Walter MacPeek*

COMPLETE OBEDIENCE

A story is told of a great captain who, after a battle, was talking over the events of the day with his officers. He asked them who had done the best that day. Some spoke of one man who had fought bravely, and some of others. "No," he said, "you are all wrong. The best man in the field today was a soldier who was just lifting an arm to strike an enemy, but when he heard the trumpet sound retreat, checked himself, and dropped his arm without striking a blow. That perfect and ready obedience to the will of his general is the noblest thing that has been done this day."

—Scouting in the L. D. S. Church

A SELECTIVE OBEDIENCE

Among the quite frequent questionable teachings of my early youth was one which said, "Always do what you're told to do."

Youth, unfortunately, is often inclined to interpret suggestions literally. Should a boy earnestly try to carry out this common precept so frequently suggested, he would find himself doing and undoing, building and tearing down, helping and hurting, and running himself about in circles. We can't obey everybody.

All about us there are orders to do this and that. Every person we meet directs us to do or to refrain from doing one thing or another.

Early in life we must learn that obedience must be a *selective* process. We must learn whom to obey, which impulse to hear, which to disregard. If we try to obey all, we become another Jekyll-Hyde with severe complications.

We must learn to *evaluate* the one who directs. We must learn to look to the *outcome* of our act.

As we grow older, we learn that obedience is more than our mere favorable response to a command. We come to realize that there is an obedience to a still higher law—an obedience to what we *know* to be right. Thus we begin to have something more than a blind response to command. We begin to develop for ourselves an understanding response to the higher law—the law of life purposefulness.

—Walter MacPeek

8

A Scout Is Cheerful

He smiles whenever he can.
His obedience to orders
. . . is prompt and cheery.
. . . He never shirks
. . . nor grumbles at hardships.

He keeps his heart and mind buoyant enough that discouragement and discontent cannot get a foothold within.

Cheerfulness is a habit, a good habit. Cheerfulness cannot live in the same house with pessimism and grouchiness; cheerfulness will kick them out!

A lady rang a doorbell and waited. Meanwhile she heard a musical voice, evidently from the cellar, ringing forth in a rollicking song, accompanied by a noise as a shoveling. She rang again. A youth came to the door and laughed, saying, "You must have been highly entertained."

"I did enjoy your music truly," she replied.

The singer explained, "You see, I don't like to shovel ashes one bit, so I always tune up when it has to be done. It seems to make the job shorter or easier someway."

AND THE DAY WAS BRIGHTER

Even so simple an act as taking a walk is a chance to spread gladness and make someone happy. Phillips Brooks, the Episcopal bishop, once went past a newspaper office in Boston on a rainy day, and the paper printed this item: "The day was dark and gloomy, but Phillips Brooks walked down Newspaper Row and all was bright."

In another city a minister on his way to the study in his church gave a cheery greeting to an elderly workman digging a ditch. "Good morning, my friend!" he called out. "How are you this glorious day?"

The laborer had seldom been greeted in such a manner by a well-dressed stranger and said in surprise, "Mister, you speak to me just like Jesus."

—W. D. *Cavert* in With Jesus
on the Scout Trail

THE WORTH OF A SMILE

Keep smiling. Smiles do an immense amount of good in this rather sad-in-spots old world. We read the other day of an unfortunate lad who came into contact with an electric wire in climbing a tree and burned his face so badly that the smile muscle was injured, and he could do nothing but twist his lips and pucker his face in sad fashion when he really wanted to smile. A damage suit was instituted against a local power and light company, and the jury returned a verdict giving the boy $20,000.

The writer who told the tale added, "If a smile is worth $20,000 when you lose it, it is worth $20,000 when you use it." Yes, and it is worth infinitely more than that in coin not made of metal. Then smile, Scouts, not only Christmas Day but everyday, when things go right and when they go wrong, whether you like your job or whether you don't. Whether the person who needs your friendly smile is friend or stranger, "A merry heart goes all the way."

—Boys' Life

SMILE ANYWAY!

Once there was a man who lost a ten-dollar bill and he went up the street grumbling and worrying and telling everybody about it as if it were the greatest trouble in the world. He met another man and told his story.

"Huh," said the other man, "you think you've got troubles. Listen. I've got six children at home in bed with measles. My wife's got a busted arm. The cook's quit. They're foreclosing a mortgage on my house today. My horse has had the blind staggers. My dog just bit a stranger in the leg and the fellow's looking for me to lick me. Troubles! Master, you're enjoying the pinnacle of good luck."

Just think that over and see if you get an idea from it.

HOW WE REACT

Do you know how a pearl is made? A grain of sand or a tiny pebble gets inside an oyster and becomes a source of annoyance or possible injury. The oyster at once defends itself by surrounding the harmful object with juices that harden it into pearl. The thing that hurts is turned into a valuable jewel.

Beauty of character is made the same way. Suppose you have been badly disappointed or face a hard situation. Perhaps someone said something that hurt your feelings or did something that was mean and spiteful. You can get mad and sulk, and make everyone around you unhappy. Or you can call forth your powers of cheerfulness and forgiveness, and cover the hurt in such a way that your life becomes stronger and happier than it was before.

—W. D. *Cavert* in WITH JESUS
ON THE SCOUT TRAIL

HAPPIFYING

"Happifying. Never heard that word before? Well, look it up in the dictionary. You can't find it? No, it's a word used by Scouts. You can guess what it means. Just this. Making people happy."

In those words Robert Baden-Powell, the founder of Scouting, greeted Boy Scouts in a letter published in *Boys' Life* magazine some years ago.

Baden-Powell went on to explain that wherever he had gone in America, he had been made happy by the enthusiasm and friendliness of Scouts and Scout leaders. He described the spick-and-span appearance of a Scout troop that saw him off as he left America. And he spoke of his unbounded optimism for the future of Scouting after having made the trip through this country.

The very word *happifying* can be a challenge to all of us. One of these days it might even be in the dictionary, if we make it a common enough concept by the way we live and treat each other, and carry on our Scouting work. It's worth trying.

WHEN THINGS GO WRONG
(Scoutmaster philosophizes on ways of looking at life)

Did you ever see a fellow who was forever thinking that people were picking on him? It's a disastrous habit to get into, yet one that is pretty common. Each of us might well say to himself, "Don't let this happen to you."

I recall one of our boys years ago who pitched his tent carelessly and it blew down on him in the middle of the night. He tried to blame someone else, but we laughed so heartily that he finally had to admit to himself, "Well, I guess it was my own fault."

Another time a boy burned a steak. "It was the fire's fault," he insisted, lashing out desperately for someone to blame, until the other fellows laughed at him and showed him how the same bed of coals could help turn out a well-cooked steak.

Things usually happen to us because we set the stage for them. Actually, people around us are too busy to spend their time picking on us. They have more important things to do.

I've got it figured out this way! When something goes wrong, the first place to look for the cause is down inside ourselves.

—Walter MacPeek

BE SURE BEFORE YOU BARK

I'm sure each one of you fellows has been in a situation, sometime or another, when you have said something which, when you found out all the facts, you wished you could take back—wished that you could retreat gracefully.

I remember hearing of an incident on one of the islands in the Pacific in World War II, when a commanding officer had lined up a company of his men to ask for volunteers to go on a mission of extreme peril. He explained the danger that they would be in and asked for anyone willing to risk his life in this way to step two paces forward.

At just that time his attention was distracted by another officer who passed a message along to him. When he turned back to his men he discovered the line still unbroken.

"What, not a single one?" he demanded and started to upbraid the men. Then he discovered that the entire line had cheerfully advanced two paces!

—THE SCOUTMASTER'S MINUTE

9

A Scout Is Thrifty

He does not wantonly
    destroy property.
He works faithfully,
... wastes nothing,
... and makes the best use
    of his opportunities.
He saves his money
... so that he may pay his own way,
    ... be generous to those in need,
    ... and helpful to worthy objects.
He may work for pay,
... but must not receive tips
... for courtesies or good turns.

"He who chops his own wood gets warmed twice," says an old proverb.

Early in life a good Scout learns something of thrift. Yet if he lives in a wasteful, destructive environment he tends to grow like the forces around him. Often he needs to guard himself against such influences. He needs to care for his clothes and to respect the property of others.

We need to recognize the values of property and, even more, the great importance of *human values*. A Scout is thrifty of all values—tangible and intangible. He is not wasteful or careless or destructive of his own or of the resources and property of others.

When the mayor of Easton, Pennsylvania, asked Cub Scout Jonathan Reibman of Pack 3 to explain the meaning of the Scout Law, "A Scout Is Thrifty," he answered, "It means you should not waste your time because you can't get it back!"

USEFULNESS

A young man asked Dr. F. W. Gunsaulus, "What am I in this world for?"

The next day the Iroquois Theater burned. This young man carried several children from the third story of the flaming theater. That day he saved twenty-eight lives.

HERITAGES

It is not that I belong to the past, but the past belongs to me. America is the youngest of the nations and inherits all that went before in history. And I am the youngest of America's children and into my hands is given all her priceless heritage, to the last great thought of the philosopher. Mine is the whole majestic past, and mine is the shining future.

—Mary Austin

PICTURE OF A BOY

The Bridge was too safe or too adventureless,
So he walked the thin and slippery log instead.
It was the log's fault that he fell in, of course.
He had been steady when the durn thing turned.
So, drying him out beside the quick woods fire we
    heard his lamentations.
"Gosh!—oh gosh!"
He didn't mind being wet, or cold, or shivering, but
    the cookies had been ruined!

—Samuel D. Bogan

EDISON'S SECRET INVENTION

A young neighbor boy darted quickly under a turnstile at Thomas Edison's summer residence and ran up to the great inventor.

"Ah-ah!" the benign old gentleman chided, "you didn't come through that gate the way a person should, now did you?"

The boy's expression sobered a little. "I'm sorry, Mr. Edison, but that thing turns too hard. My father says it's funny that with all your inventions you haven't figured out a way to make a turnstile go around any easier than that one does."

There was a twinkle in Thomas Edison's eyes as he bent down and said in a confidential tone, "I'm going to let you in on a secret, Son. I hope your father doesn't find this out, but everybody who comes through that turnstile pumps a gallon of water into the tank on my roof!"

—G. E. C.

HE FOUND OUT

William Henry Perkin's father was a contractor and wanted his son to be an architect. But William had his heart set on becoming a chemist. He was so enthusiastic in his studies that he spent all his spare time in the laboratory.

Fortunately, he was too young and energetic to take "no" for an answer. The scientists of his day all said that quinine couldn't be made in the laboratory. William thought he would try it anyway. His attempts to make synthetic quinine were a failure, but during his experiments he accidentally mixed two chemicals and found that a purple dye resulted.

William Perkin was just eighteen years old at the time, but he took out a patent and built a factory to manufacture dye from coal tar. His accidental discovery led to modern pigments. Since then, fabric dye, ink, saccharin, perfume, and cosmetics have been developed from coal tar.

—W. G. in Boys' Life

THRIFTY JASPER

Mathematics was not Jasper's strong point, and during an examination he was given this problem:

"If one horse can run one mile in a minute and a half, and another horse can do the same distance in two minutes, how far ahead would the first horse be if they ran a race of two miles at their respective speeds?"

Jasper worried over this for some time, and then thought of a way out.

"I regret to say," he wrote, "that I cannot deal with this problem, as my parents have always told me never to have anything to do with horse racing in any form."

—Our Dumb Animals

A SENSE OF PRIDE

"I'd sooner wear ten merit badges that I've earned with flying colors than to have twenty that I just got by on," a Scout told me one day. I agreed with him and I'm sure you do, too.

Merit badges help you explore your world. They

help you build your world larger. They help you reach out your horizons.

Earning merit badges also helps you to make new friends, to get acquainted with high-grade men who serve as merit badge counselors. Naturally you'll want them to respect you, and you'll do a reasonable job of preparation.

I know that each one of you wants to have a sense of pride in the merit badges you earn. You want to do your level best to qualify for them the best you can. They'll mean more to you that way.

—Walter MacPeek

KEEPING AT IT

Benjamin Disraeli was a great English statesman, remembered today for many things that he did and said.

Here is a quotation worth thinking of every once in a while. Disraeli once asked the question, "Have you ever watched a stonecutter at work?" and went on to explain, "He will hammer away at a rock for perhaps a hundred times without a crack showing in it. Then on the hundred and first blow the rock will split in two. It is not that blow alone, that one hundred and first blow, that accomplished the result, but the hundred others that went before it as well."

Each of us is sometimes discouraged at how long it takes to learn something, and how long it takes to become proficient. Remember that every time you work on something, and every effort you put into the task will count sooner or later.

Recall the one hundred and one blows, each of them important in breaking the rock and in reaching your goal. Persistence pays off.

—*Walter MacPeek*

PURSUIT

Perhaps you've heard the story of a disgruntled acquaintance who came to Benjamin Franklin one day and complained about the Constitution of the United States.

"Where is all the happiness it's supposed to guarantee us? Look at the bickering, the injustice, and poverty in the world," the man said.

Franklin smiled broadly at the complaining man and replied, "All the Constitution of the United States guarantees, my friend, is the *pursuit* of happiness. You have to catch up with it yourself."

There are people who go around in life complaining and claiming that they have a right to everything. We have a right to work for things, not to demand them. We have a right to pursue happiness. We have a right to make ourselves count in these situations. But we had better not sit around like birds with our mouths wide open expecting the world to bring its choice bits to us. Such things just don't happen that way. We've got to go after things if we really want them.

Our Constitution guarantees us the privilege of the *pursuit* of happiness.

—*Walter MacPeek*

A SCOUT OF EARLY DAYS

Picture a camping trip in incessant spring showers. Then imagine that you are on a trek into wilderness country in early spring, not merely for fun but for the serious purpose of surveying land. Add to this picture of hardships the natural handicap of a pioneer setting of two hundred years ago.

No matches. No convenient canned food. No snug waterproof sleeping bags. The tents of the party of which young George Washington was a member, on that first exploration of the Shenandoah Valley, were unceremoniously blown down by violent winds. Somehow the elements are no respecters either of a boy of great promise or of a future president!

On this trip young Washington sought shelter in the open, as he records in his diary "under a straw house."

You should feel a thrill of common pride when you master your cooking requirement, thrilled by the knowledge that George Washington passed that

108

test, too. On that first surveying party each man did his own cooking. They used forked sticks over the fire and large chips for plates.

We know that in his youth, George Washington shared with you in these bits of Scoutcraft: signaling, tracking, use of knife and hatchet, fire building, cooking, thrift, use of compass, safety practice, Scoutlike living, swimming, hiking, map making and reading, handicraft, judging, and nature knowledge. There really isn't much that we do today that Washington, as a boy, didn't do—and do remarkably well!

—Walter MacPeek

TOMORROW

I suppose it's natural for fellows of Scout age to try to make the best of every day. I imagine if I should ask you to name your best day, you would answer very much like a famous Danish sculptor when he was asked about his favorite creation.

His name was Thorvaldsen and people frequently asked him about his favorite bits of work, what pattern his technique followed, and questions of that kind. One day he was asked a slightly different question: "Which do you consider your greatest statue?" Thorvaldsen answered promptly with a smile, "The next one."

I suppose this might be true for every one of us.

109

If I should ask you what day of all your life you consider most important and most significant, the one that you are going to do your very best with, you and many other Scouts would probably answer "tomorrow."

Good luck in making your tomorrows count for a great deal for yourself and your world.

—*Walter MacPeek*

10

A Scout Is Brave

He has the courage
. . . to face danger in spite of fear,
. . . and to stand up for the right
. . . against the coaxings of friends
. . . or the jeers or threats of enemies,
. . . and defeat does not down him.

What better statement could blueprint the coura-geous attitude of a good Scout than, "He has the courage to face danger in spite of fear, and to stand for the right against the coaxings of friends and the jeers of enemies, and defeat does not down him"?

That part of the law is worth knowing so well that we can repeat it to ourselves in times of tension, when we feel need for personal reinforcement.

The brave find a home in every land.   —*Ovid*

We come to know best what men are, in their worst jeopardies.   —*Daniel*

The brave man is not he who feels no fear, for that were stupid and irrational; but he whose noble soul its fear subdues, and bravely dares the danger which it shrinks from.   —*Joanna Baillie*

Courage is adversity's lamp.   —*Vauvenargues*

Courage makes a man more than himself; for he is then himself plus his valor.   —*W. R. Alger*

It is in great danger that we see great courage.
—*Regnod*

He has not learned the lesson of life who does not every day surmount a fear.   —*Emerson*

THE MAN WHO OVERCAME

Theodore Roosevelt had weak eyes all his life and became a successful hunter, an omnivorous reader, and a keen naturalist. Men with defective hearing will remember that Theodore Roosevelt lost the use of one of his ears and could still distinguish calls of birds and lead a people magnificently. Men stricken with pain will remember that once Theodore Roosevelt worked at his correspondence until he fainted and the couch on which he lay was drenched with blood. Cripples will hear the words that Theodore Roosevelt spoke when a physician told him in

112

the last month of his life that he might be confined to his chair the rest of his days. "All right! I can live that way too!" The millions will remember the inspiring leader, but the few with grim terrors to face will always cherish most *the man who overcame.*

—TRUE STORIES OF REAL SCOUTS

KNOWING HOW AND FOLLOWING THROUGH

This is a true story about what happened to a family in Muskogee, Oklahoma.

It was winter, very cold, and on this particular morning a gas heater had been lighted to warm the little group while they were dressing. They were playing around, as young children do, and one of them thoughtlessly stepped too close to the gas heater. In a moment her flimsy nightclothes were a mass of flames! The little girl shrieked and the other children began to cry. The mother came running and stood filled with horror. The father and thirteen-year-old son came dashing up the stairs. The son was a Boy Scout and in his troop he had often practiced, as a part of his first-aid training, responding to just such accidents. Almost automatically he caught up a small rug from the floor and rolled his shrieking little sister in its enveloping folds. In a moment he had smothered the flames and prevented serious injury.

The next day the father told the boy's Scoutmaster about what had happened and said, "Thank God my son is a Scout and has learned first aid! He knew what to do while I stood helplessly confused."

—*James E. West* in
MAKING THE MOST OF YOURSELF

ANOTHER SCOUT HERO

In a disastrous hurricane off Bermuda, the *Eastway* was one of the many vessels which foundered.

Foot by foot the water crept up the metal plates of her holds. From a tiny cabin somewhere in the interior of the ship, the wireless operator sent forth the appeal to every vessel on the seven seas. Dot-dot-dot! Dash-dash-dash! Dot-dot-dot . . . SOS! SOS! SOS!

The last of the ship's boats was lowered and the remaining few members of the crew climbed in. They called to the wireless operator. It was the last of the boats, and the *Eastway* was doomed. But the operator heard not. Had he not his duty to fulfill? SOS! SOS! SOS! He must not desert his post.

With a shudder the *Eastway* lifted her bow to the sky and plunged down.

Who was the wireless operator? Only a Scout—Ralph Janes—member of the First Lehighton Buzzard Troop. Perhaps, as he sank beneath the waves,

he might have been heard to murmur, "I promise
to do my duty . . ."   —THE SCOUT, *London*

YOUR HERITAGE

Your heritage is a far-flung one. From explorers,
pioneers, inventors, scientists, writers, thinkers, and
others, many values have come to you. They have
helped to provide the inheritance that you enjoy.
You need to value this heritage highly.

Your Scouting heritage goes back, of course, to
Baden-Powell and to the founding of the Boy Scouts
of America in 1910. Many men have contributed to
the Scouting which you enjoy today. Through the
years Scouting has grown richer and more meaningful.

As many men have given of themselves and their
talents for you, you in return can do something to
enrich and improve the Scouting that will be possible
for generations that will follow you.

—*Walter MacPeek*

MESSAGE CARRIERS

More than fifty years have passed since the famous
message was carried to Garcia. But important messages have been carried frequently during those many
years. They're still being carried. Maybe tomorrow

one of you will carry some kind of message to Garcia.

What does it take? What are the difficulties involved? First, you must get started. Then you must keep going and, most important of all, you *must get there*. It's as simple as that.

Can you think of some Americans who have carried messages. Yes, there was Paul Revere and Caesar Rodney. Yes, Lewis and Clark might be classified as message carriers although they did more than that. Usually message carriers open the way for others to follow.

In an army a scout is one who goes ahead of the group, finding and opening the way for others to follow. So we can be message carriers, and more, we can scout the new areas; we can open the trails for others to follow.

—*Walter MacPeek*

SCOUT COURAGE

If they told Eddie Spain that his polio attack would keep him from doing the things other boys did, Eddie wasn't listening. For Eddie went right ahead and learned to play the cornet, skate, ride a bike, carry a paper route, and become a Star Scout in Troop 94, Salem, Illinois.

When the troop hiked the Illinois-Lincoln trail

from New Salem State Park to Springfield—a distance of twenty-one miles—Eddie hiked the first ten miles without crutches and finished on crutches.

Tough going? Sure. But he made it—and went fishing the next day! He went fishing alone, though. The other fellows were exhausted.

THE KNIGHT OF TODAY

> I envy not the Knight of old
>   Who lived for honor true,
> Who rode away to distant lands
>   His Great Good Turn to do.
>
> I envy not the soldiers brave
>   Who kept our country free.
> For chances here will prove my strength,
>   They'll ever challenge me.
>
> I shall not long for days gone by,
>   My chance to serve is here.
> And with my motto "Be Prepared"
>   My duty's written clear.
>   —Walter MacPeek

HE DID WHAT WAS NEEDED

Sea Explorer William Shaefer, on board the Sea Exporer Ship *Ranger* was checking its mooring lines when he heard a cry and saw a young man, Richard Blaser, floundering in the murky water of Lockport

117

Locks on the Illinois Waterway. The victim was behind the propellers of a barge pusher, in danger of being sucked in. Running along the tow of barges, to which the *Ranger* was moored, William saw him go under once, then bob to the surface, flailing his arms in the air. Just as William was abreast of Richard a fellow Explorer threw the drowning man a life ring, but it went beyond his reach and the current was taking it farther away. William leaped into the water fully clothed, swam to the life ring, and thrust it into the hands of the desperate man. He then used the life ring to tow the victim to a barge where both were pulled on board.

HE WAS PREPARED

Charles Bappert, a twelve-year-old Second Class Scout, was helping a friend on a paper route in Lansing, Michigan. When he saw smoke coming from the Balog residence, he ran into the house, telephoned the fire department, and shouted a warning through the house. Joyce Balog, on the second floor, was awakened by his warning and groped her way from the burning building.

RESCUE

Star Scout Stephen Forsstrom was riding his bicycle on a hill near the Emerson School in Spokane,

Washington. He saw Gerald Kildare, eleven, take a long skid on his bicycle and fall on his side, scraping his head and hip on the rough road. Gerald lay with his face in the mud. The Scout found him breathing with difficulty. He forced his index finger and thumb into the injured boy's mouth, freeing his tongue, and removed dirt and broken teeth that were obstructing his breathing. Stephen then sent for help and the injured boy was soon on the way to the hospital.

IN A TOUGH SPOT

After a day of duck hunting in the Mississippi River marshland not far from Weaver, Minnesota, Eagle Scout Jerry Foster was putting his gear away, preparing to return home, when he heard cries of distress from the river. There are many stumps and deadheads in this area, and the channel is difficult to locate even in daylight. With a companion he headed his motorboat into the darkness in search of the persons in trouble.

After considerable searching they found two men, standing a mile from shore in icy water up to their chins. Their capsized boat was nearby. They were unable to move because of the mud and danger of getting into deeper water. Jerry and his companion pulled the victims into his boat, righted the capsized boat, and towed it to safety through the pitch-dark, cold, and choppy water.

KNOW-HOW AND BRAVERY

Kenneth O'Steen, twelve-year-old Tenderfoot of only a few months' experience, was working on a farm near Cross Creek, Florida. Kenneth saw a tractor out of control, driven by his employer Dr. Harry Evans. Rushing to the scene he found Dr. Evans had been thrown to the ground and run over by tractor and mower. His legs were broken and parts of his body crushed.

Kenneth did what he could to ease the pain, then ran to the farmhouse to send for aid. He returned with a supply of water and a tarpaulin to shield the injured man from the sun and stayed with him until an ambulance and a doctor arrived. The report of the accident states, "We believe that Dr. Evans is alive today because Scout O'Steen was there to care for him."

11

A Scout Is Clean

He keeps clean
...in body
...and thought,
...stands for clean speech,
...clean sports,
...clean habits,
...and travels with a clean crowd.

We just naturally take on something of the color of our surroundings. Everything we touch and see and think has some effect on us. Accordingly, we choose consciously where we go, whom we travel with, and what we read and think and admire.

Horace wrote: "Unless the vessel is clean, whatever you pour into it turns sour."

An old proverb says: "One keep-clean is better than ten make-cleans."

A father, wishing to show his son the effect of habit in his life, sent him for a hammer and a nail which he deliberately drove into the parlor table. It went in with ease. Then handing the hammer to his son he said: "Now, my son, pull it out." After a great deal of effort and much marring of the table, the nail was removed. Then the father said to his son, "Now, my son, pull out the hole," adding, "Habits can be pulled out, but their effects, never."

A BOY WALKED DOWN THE STREET

We were walking down the street. At almost every stop we could not help noticing that some misguided or unguided child with a piece of chalk had scribbled indecent phrases on the sidewalk.

A fine-looking, strongly built, well-dressed boy was walking a few paces in front of us. Something about him had attracted my attention. He gave the impression, merely by his stride, of going somewhere, of being intensely in earnest.

Once he paused, his eye resting upon the scribbling on the sidewalk. He seemed hurt that any child in his town would stoop to such a thing. Then, sliding the sole of his shoe back and forth on the cement, he erased the words. As he went on he paused here and there to obliterate a word or phrase.

And walking along behind him, my friend and I

followed his example. We, too, used the soles of our shoes to erase the marks. Behind us came several boys. Realizing the manliness of the example of the young man up ahead, they also joined in the task.

A few days later I saw one of those same boys again erasing similar chalk marks. Without a spoken word that one young man's character, his sensitiveness and his repulsion at vulgarity and indecency, had started an informal campaign of cleanliness.

Think of the contagion of his example! And now, day after day, perhaps all down through the ages, that unspoken example will carry on, because a boy walked down the street.

—Walter MacPeek

WASHINGTON'S INFLUENCE

George Washington was no sissy, but he did not like to hear people swear. When he asked a group of officers to have dinner with him and one of them used profane language, the general quietly reproved the man by saying, "I supposed I had invited only gentlemen to dine with me." So strongly did Washington feel about swearing among his soldiers that in July, 1776, he issued a general order in which he described it as "foolish and wicked—a vice so mean and low, without any temptation, that every man of sense and character detests and despises it." He

123

called upon the officers to check it "by example as well as by influence."

—W. D. *Cavert* in With Jesus
on the Scout Trail

STOPPED SHORT

Up in the north woods two old prospectors lived about ten miles from each other. At intervals they would break the monotony of their lonely existence by visiting each other. On one particular occasion, during a visit, one old fellow turned to the other and said, "I got one of them cookery books once, but I never could do nothing with it."

"Too much fancy stuff in it, eh?" said his friend.

"No, that ain't it," replied the first prospector. "It's just that every one of them recipes began the same way—'Take a clean dish'—and that stops me."

—Boys' Life

DOING SOMETHING ABOUT TRASH

"The Boy Scouts of this area request you not to litter the woods with trash. Please take your rubbish to the dump." That's the positive wording of signs posted by Troop 2, Corning, New York, in the Spencer Hill section about a half mile from the city limits. The troop spends a Saturday morning three or four times a year in this service to the community.

124

CLEAN-MINDED

It's what goes on in a boy's mind that's important. He most likely will become a strong, clean-thinking man if his thoughts get started right. He's likely to be something else if they don't.

The boy really can't help his thoughts very much. Impressions, contacts, surroundings start them. The first simple things he sees and does, in earliest youth, set him thinking. Soon he's thinking fast—good, clean thoughts or ugly, distorted ones, depending on where and how he's headed.

In many homes boys are not thinking right. Mother doesn't know it; dad doesn't suspect. Home conditions are "good." Isn't there a lot of fine furniture and good food and a radio and a library full of books? What if dad *is* worried about business and hasn't much time to talk to boys? What if mother is busy with her own affairs? Isn't the house well furnished, the boys well fed, books to read, and a radio to fool with?

All these things may not keep a boy thinking right. If they don't, then slowly, insidiously, wrong thoughts eat into the boy's character as surely as termites eat into the timbers in our buildings. So men have arranged to get boys together, under wise leadership, to keep them thinking right. The way to do that, of course, is to keep them acting right—

doing things, good things, that are clean and wholesome and body building. A busy mind in a busy body
is likely to be a healthy mind; and a healthy mind is
likely to think straight.

—Milwaukee Journal

THE SOURCE

Not far from the city of Geneva, Switzerland, the
Arve, which is a muddy river, joins the sparkling
water of the Rhone. For a long distance after they
come together they flow along as though they were
two rivers in one channel. The clear Rhone is sharp-
ly marked off from the dull-gray Arve. How is it
that the Rhone is able to keep itself from being
sullied by the muddy water? It is because it rises at
a great height in the Alps and is fed by snow from
a glacier ten thousand feet high. The water rushes
down the mountain and then flows through the
valley so swiftly that the Arve cannot affect it.

—W. D. Cavert in With Jesus
on the Scout Trail

SIR GALAHAD'S STRENGTH

From days of the early Christian Church come
stories based on the search for the Holy Grail, which
was the cup from which Jesus and his disciples drank
at the first Lord's Supper. According to the legend

it had been brought to England by Joseph of Arimathea. Then it disappeared because of the sinfulness of the people and could be found only by one whose heart was pure. The knights of King Arthur's Round Table went far and wide in search of it, but it remained for Sir Galahad to succeed in the quest and to be made king of the city where it was kept. In Tennyson's poem Galahad described the source of his superior strength by saying:

> My good blade carves the casques of men,
> My tough lance thrusteth sure,
> My strength is as the strength of ten,
> Because my heart is pure.

—W. D. Cavert in WITH JESUS
ON THE SCOUT TRAIL

12

A Scout Is Reverent

He is reverent toward God.
He is faithful in his religious duties
...and respects
...the convictions of others
...in matters of custom
...and religion.

How do we grow in reverence? How can we feel more strongly the close presence of God? Through worship, through reverence, through faithfulness in our own church life and personal outreach to God.

We gain strength through reaching out to the Great Source of all strength.

"A man devoid of religion is like a horse without a bridle."   —*Latin Proverb*

"You may discover tribes of men without policy, or laws, or cities, or any of the arts of life; but nowhere will you find them without some form of religion."   —*Blair*

"I have now disposed of all my property to my family. There is one thing more I wish I could give them, and that is the Christian religion. If they had that, and I had not given them one shilling, they would have been rich; and if they had not that, and I had given them all the world, they could be poor."

—Patrick Henry

A SCOUT IS REVERENT

Fellows, you're a great gang for action. You like to be on the move. You play hard and work hard. You make a lot of noise sometimes. That's O.K. You're boys, and noise and action are a part of boyhood. But there's something more.

Sometimes it's good for us to find a quiet spot, such as the top of the hill under the big oak at camp. Each one of us likes to sit quietly sometimes and wonder and dream and weigh things.

Last week as I thought of the phrase "Onward for God and My Country," I kept thinking about you fellows. Each of us is going onward. That's our direction. We've got the steam, and we're heading in the right direction.

We look to God for help, for strength. He helps us and guides us.

And, of course, about the best thing we can do for our country is to be the kind of fellow who, if he is multiplied by two hundred million, will help make our country an even better place than it is today.

Many people have dreamed of America as a place where people can be at their best. Part of the dream has already been worked out, but some of it still waits for us to translate into action.

—Scoutmaster's Minute

GOD'S FIDDLE

A story is told of a conversation between a businessman and Sir Harry Lauder, the famous Scotch comedian. "I want to thank you for all the happiness you have given me, Sir Harry," the man remarked. "I have looked forward to your American performances as one of the real joys of my life."

Harry Lauder without any thought of jesting responded, "Don't thank me, laddie. God put something into me that seems to give pleasure to many thousands of people," he said. "What it is I don't know, nor where it came from, nor when it may go. I don't seem to control it—it seems to control me. Thank it, whatever it is—not me."

—True Stories of Real Scouts

GOD'S LITTLE WORKSHOP

George Washington Carver, a slave boy who was once exchanged for a horse, became one of the world's greatest scientists. He taught science at Tuskegee Normal and Industrial Institute in Alabama for a salary of fifteen hundred dollars a year and refused to leave when he was offered fifty thousand dollars a year by Thomas A. Edison. Why did he stay at Tuskegee? Because his great desire was to help the poor people of the South. Through his experiments he found hundreds of new ways to use peanuts and sweet potatoes, and so increased the incomes of underpaid Southern farmers.

Over the door of his laboratory he put the sign, "God's Little Workshop." He never claimed any special credit for his work but humbly thought of himself as one to whom the Creator was revealing his secrets.

—*W. D. Cavert* in With Jesus
on the Scout Trail

FELLOWSHIP WITH GOD

When you go to Boston, be sure to see the statue outside the art museum. It shows an Indian sitting on his pony. The horse has its eyes half closed and its head hanging down, but the rider is gazing upward and has his arms thrown back in prayer to the Great Spirit. The sculptor has tried to show the difference between an animal, which has no sense of reverence, and a man, who is able to have fellowship with God.

—W. D. Cavert in WITH JESUS
ON THE SCOUT TRAIL

LETTER TO CAMP DIRECTOR

He means so very much to us,
This boy of ours you borrow.
He's everything we have,
Sole gift to the Tomorrow.

We gladly loan him to you
For we know at Camp he'll grow.
You'll find him ever eager,
There's much he wants to know.

We know you'll treat him kindly
As he explores the hills;
And fills his heart with wonder,
And fills his day with thrills.

But most of all we pray you,
Please do not think us odd—
We hope at camp he'll practice
Close fellowship with God.
—Walter MacPeek

LINCOLN'S PRAYER

Abe Lincoln's prayer for a sick boy in a covered wagon, on his way west with his parents to establish

132

a new home: "O God, the Father of all living, I ask you to look with gentle mercy upon this little boy, lying sick in this covered wagon. His people are traveling far, to seek a home in the wilderness, to do your work, God, to make this earth a good place for your children to live in. They can see clearly where they're going, and they're not afraid to face all the perils that lie along the way. I humbly beg you not to take their child from them. Grant him the freedom of life. Do not condemn him to the imprisonment of death. Do not deny him his birthright. Let him know the sight of great plains and high mountains, of green valleys and wide rivers. For this little boy is an American, and these things belong to him and he to them. Spare him that he too may strive for the ideals for which his fathers have labored so faithfully and so long. Spare him and give him his father's strength—give us all strength, O God, to do the work that is before us."

LISTENING TO GOD'S VOICE

Joan of Arc heard voices from God calling her to become the leader of the French army and to free her country from its enemies. She secured an interview with King Charles and told him about her message from God. The king said that if the voices had anything to say for the welfare of France, they

should speak to him, for he was the king. Joan
replied, "They do come to you, but you do not hear
them. If you prayed from your heart and listened,
you would hear the voices as well as I."

—W. D. *Cavert* in WITH JESUS
ON THE SCOUT TRAIL

CADET PRAYER

O God, our Father, thou Searcher of men's
hearts, help us to draw near to thee in sincerity and
truth. May our religion be filled with gladness and
may our worship of thee be natural.

Strengthen and increase our admiration for honest
dealing and clean thinking, and suffer not our hatred
of hypocrisy and pretense ever to diminish. Encourage us in our endeavor to live above the common
level of life. Make us choose the harder right instead
of the easier wrong, and never to be content with a
half truth when the whole can be won.

Endow us with courage that is born of loyalty to
all that is noble and worthy, that scorns to compro-
mise with vice and injustice and knows no fear when
truth and right are in jeopardy. Guard us against
flippancy and irreverence in the sacred things of life.
Grant us new ties of friendship and new opportunities of service.

Kindle our hearts in fellowship with those of a

cheerful countenance, and soften our hearts with sympathy for those who sorrow and suffer. May we find genuine pleasure in clean and wholesome mirth and feel inherent disgust for all coarse-minded humor.

Help us in our work and in our play to keep ourselves physically strong, mentally awake, and morally straight, that we may the better maintain the honor of the Corps, untarnished and unsullied, and acquit ourselves like men in our effort to realize the ideals of West Point in doing our duty to thee and to our country. All of which we ask in the name of the great Friend and Master of men. Amen.

—*Written by Colonel Clayton E. Wheat,*
  Professor of English, United States
  Military Academy at West Point

ONE GOD AND FATHER

The stillness of a clear, sunny Sunday morning was broken as Train 213, with Boy Scout Jamboree banners from New York and New Jersey, pulled onto a spur track in front of our home in Vista, Pennsylvania and came to a stop.

The doors opened and over four hundred Scouts and leaders poured out, headed in what appeared to be every direction. But quickly, as the other members of my family and I watched in awe at the heart-warming spectacle, three groups formed. In the center, at an altar erected on the steps of the train, a priest clad in white and gold was conducting a field Mass. Over across the road was another service where chaplain and Scouts kept their hats on, which told us that here was a Jewish service. From a grassy slope boyish voices swelled in a grand, holy hymn, as a song leader and a chaplain led a Protestant service.

Our hearts were stirred as we noted that every member of the train crew had joined in the worship. The brakeman at the end of the train and the engineer, at their posts, were kneeling in reverence as they watched.

Then the brief services were over, Scouts quietly filed back into the coaches, and the group was once more on its way. As the train began to roll the engineer gave a couple of short blasts on the whistle. It seemed to us as we watched in hushed silence that he was saying "amen" to this stirring demonstration of faith and of understanding. And our hearts echoed a fervent "amen."   —Scouting

TWELVE TINY LETTERS

Can you all see what this is, fellows? That's right. It's a Lincoln penny. If you have one with you, take it out of your pocket and let's take a look at it. What do you find on it? Yes, that's right. Just above

Lincoln's head in twelve tiny letters are the words "In God we trust." Not only as individuals, but as a nation, too, we are committed to trying to live and work in harmony with God and with his plan.

This month, all over America, Scouts are thinking often of these men who are frequently called "February's Giants." Washington, born more than 200 years ago; Lincoln, born more than 150 years ago; and Baden-Powell, born in England more than 100 years ago. These men had many things in common—love of the out-of-doors, human kindliness and love of people, and an earnest vigor in working with God in helping to work out a better world. Each of these Giants often acknowledged his dependence on God. Each gave himself without reserve in helping to carry out his will.

Twelve little letters on our humblest coin—*In God we trust.*

—Boy Scout Program Quarterly

NATIONAL LEADERS AND PRAYER

There is on the Subtreasury Building in New York City a fine piece of statuary of George Washington at Valley Forge, kneeling in prayer in the woods in winter. That figure explains a great deal of the strength of Washington's life. It is no accident that the two greatest Americans whom we all look up to

137

and most admire, Washington and Lincoln, were men of prayer and men of faith in God. Their strong belief in God was the rudder which guided the ship.

—*H. E. Luccock*

WITH GOD'S HELP

"Don't get the idea that I won this race on my own. The Lord helped me," said Gilbert Dodds, champion runner, after one of his brilliant victories on the track. In spite of his fame as an athlete "Galloping Gil" is humble instead of conceited, for he knows that speed and endurance are qualities that have been given him by God and not merely developed by himself.

His faith in God makes Gil a strong believer in prayer. He is said never to let a day go by without kneeling to thank God for his blessings and to ask for divine help. Before each race he always prayed, not that he might be the winner, but that God would give him strength to do his best.

—W. *D. Cavert* in WITH JESUS
ON THE SCOUT TRAIL

A BOY'S REVERENCE

A steady stream of profane words poured from the lips of a wealthy man who was looking at the vases and dishes in the shop of the English potter

Josiah Wedgwood. The potter was a sincere Christian and was worried over the influence the man's swearing might have on a boy who worked in the shop and stood nearby. Picking up his most beautiful vase, Wedgwood threw it on the floor and broke it in pieces. "Why did you smash such a priceless object?" asked the amazed visitor.

"There are other things worth more than vases," replied Wedgwood. "I can make another vase as good as that one, but you never can be sure that a boy's reverence, once destroyed, will be regained."

—*W. D. Cavert* in With Jesus
on the Scout Trail

SOURCE OF STRENGTH

I sought for advice and guidance
    For I was confused and blue
Where could I find good counsel?
    Despairing I came to you.

I had sought out a lawyer learned;
    He had talked at wearying length.
I became more confused and baffled
    I found there no source of strength.

Then I consulted a doctor nearby,
    He examined me with greatest of skill.
Yet I came away from his office,
    Still baffled, confused, and ill.

139

At last in longing I knelt,
  And poured out my heart to Him
Recalling misfortune and failure,
  My defeat and my hopes now so dim.

Then, relieved, I promised Him truly
  Once again I'd do my part.
He is the friend who truly strengthens,
  He listens with the kindest heart.
                —Walter MacPeek

A PARTNERSHIP

"Who made you?" the church school teacher asked a boy in his class.

"God made me," the boy replied quickly, "but I'm not finished yet!"

How vividly that answer presents the situation! God made me and placed me in the world, and he continues to guide me and help me. But he depends upon me, too, and expects my cooperation.

And as the boy said, "I'm not finished yet."
                —Walter MacPeek

STOP FRETTING AND START WORKING WITH GOD

Unhappy people, especially the worriers, fretters, complainers, can become happy, confident people when they once start to take themselves in hand.

When they make a beginning in really believing in people and working earnestly as a cooperator with God in helping to shape the everyday events around them, they then discover that they become different people.

When people stop fretting and begin using that formerly wasted energy in building faith in people and in working out a cooperative relationship with God, they discover a new zest for living and a new purpose in life. —*Walter MacPeek*

AN INDIAN TRANSLATION OF THE TWENTY-THIRD PSALM

The Great Father above is a Shepherd Chief, and I am his, and with him I want not. He throws out to me a rope, and the name of the rope is love. He draws me, and he draws me, and he draws me to where the grass is green and the water is not dangerous, and I eat and lie down satisfied.

Sometimes my heart is very weak and falls down, but he lifts it up again and draws me into a good road. His name is wonderful. Sometime, it may be very soon, it may be longer, it may be a long, long time, he will draw me into a place between mountains. It is dark there, but I will not draw back. I will not be afraid, for it is in there between these mountains that the Shepherd will meet me; and the

141

hunger I have felt in my heart all through this life will be satisfied. Sometimes he makes the love rope into a whip, but afterwards he gives me a staff that I may lean on.

He spreads a table before me with all kinds of food. He puts his hand upon my head—all "tired" is gone. My cup he fills until it runs over.

What I tell you is true. I lie not. These roads that are away ahead will stay with me through life, and afterwards I will go to live in the Big Tepee, and sit down with the Shepherd Chief forever.

—*Author Unknown*

INDEX

American Dream, 115
Austin, Mary, 102

Baden-Powell, 62, 98
Bill from mother, 45
Bogan, Samuel D., 103
Bravery, 111
Brimhall, G. H., 37
Brooks, E. S., 26
Brooks, Phillips, 87, 95
Burden, 43

Cadet prayer, 134
Camp director, letter to, 132
Cavert, Walter D., 17, 43, 65, 82, 88, 95, 97, 124, 126, 127, 132, 134, 138, 139
Cheerfulness, 94
Cheley, F. H., 72
Citizenship, 41
Cleanliness, 121, 125
Coombs, Frank E. L., 85
Corning, N. Y., Troop 2, 124
Courage, 57, 116

Courtesy, 69, 70
Cub Scout, 78

Dickinson, Emily, 77
Disraeli, Benjamin, 106

Earning the right, 41
Edison, Thomas, 103
Emerson, Ralph Waldo, 87, 112

Faithfulness, 31
False rumor, 56
Faris, John T., 75
Franklin, Benjamin, 73, 107
Friendliness, 55, 63

Garibaldi, 82
God, working with, 130, 131, 140
Greyfriar's Bobby, 31
Gunsaulus, F. W., 102

Happifying, 98
Helpfulness, 42
Henry, Patrick, 129
Heritage, 115
Hunt, W. Ben, 63

143

Ice rescue, 85
Indian translation, 141

Jackson, Stonewall, 88

Kindness, 76
Knight of Today, 117

Lincoln's kindness, 77, 80
Lincoln's Prayer, 132
Listening to God, 133
Loyalty, 27, 29
Luccock, H. E., 138

McKenzie, David, 66
Merit badges, 51, 105
Message carriers, 115

Nickname, 58

Obedience, 87, 92
Our Dumb Animals, 33, 78, 80, 105

Patriotic gift, 29
Peale, Norman Vincent, 57
Pierson, E. F., 49
Pioneer days, 28
Prayer, 132, 141
Pride in work, 22, 51

Retlaw, M., 61
Reverence, 128, 135
Rockefeller, John D., 18
Roosevelt, Theodore, 16, 28, 112

Rope splicer champion, 90

Scholarships, 49
Scout Hero, 113, 114
Sea Explorer, 117
Sharing, 37
Sherman, Frank Dempster, 56
Smile, 95, 96
Spartans, 70
Stealing, 16
Strength, source of, 139
Strong, Marcus, 29

Thrift, 101
Traditions, 70
Trustworthy, 15, 19
Truthfulness, 23

Valley Forge, 33

Washington, D.C., Troop 8, 70
Washington, George, 24, 108, 123
"We" spirit, 39
Webb, Art, 24
Wellington, 89
Wheat, Col. C. E., 135
White, James Terry, 89

Yakima, Washington, Troop 20, 81

144